THE **ABCs** OF LEARNING ISSUES

DANA STAHL, M.ED.

EDUCATIONAL
ALTERNATIVES

PALMICHE
PRESS

© 2018 Educational Alternatives, LLC

Image & Photo Credits: Page 5 (chime meditation) © 2014 Kristina Marcelli Sargent/kristinamarcelli. wordpress.com, (yoga) © 2015 Wave Break Media(Sean Prior)/DepositPhotos.com; page 8 © 2017 Monkey-Business/DepositPhotos.com; page 9 © 2016 HighwayStarz(Ian Allenden)/DepositPhotos.com; page 11 © 2015 MidoSemsem(Mohamed Osama)/DepositPhotos.com; page 14 © 2015 Yaruta(Igor Yaruta)/DepositPhotos.com; page 16 © 2017 yacobchuk1(Viacheslov Lacobchuk)/DepositPhotos.com; page 18 © 2011 fredgreenhat(Torsten Schon)/DepositPhotos.com; page 19 © 2015 rawpixel(Robert Churchill)/DepositPhotos.com; page 20 © 2018 Palmiche Press; page 22 © 2015 gpointstudio(Anna Bizoń)/DepositPhotos.com; page 24 © 2015 Wave Break Media(Sean Prior)/DepositPhotos.com; page 25 © 2015 mkoudis(Maria Bell)/DepositPhotos.com; page 26 © 2015 Zara Muzafarova/DepositPhotos.com; page 30 © 2015 Vaicheslav(Vyacheslav Nikolaenko)/ DepositPhotos.com; page 33 © 2015 fiftycents(Marzky Ragma Jr)/DepositPhotos.com; page 36 © 2015 Artur Verkhovetskiy/DepositPhotos.com; page 44 © 2015 rawpixel(Robert Churchill)/DepositPhotos.com; page 47 © 2017 Palmiche Press; page 48 © 2017 Palmiche Press; page 49 © 2015 Fer Gregory/DepositPhotos.com; page 51 © 2015 sokolfly(Artem Sokol)/DepositPhotos.com; page 62 © 2015 blueringmedia(Daniel Cole)/Deposit-Photos.com; page 66 © 2015 Igor Tishenko/DepositPhotos.com; page 67 © 2015 SSilver(Leigh Prather)/ DepositPhotos.com; page 68 © 2015 sindler1(Attila Sindler)/DepositPhotos.com; page 72 © 2015 chones (Stoycho Stoychev)/DepositPhotos.com; page 75 © 2015 boggy22(Goran Bogicevic)/DepositPhotos.com; page 80 © 2014 deskcube/DepositPhotos.com; page 81 © 2015 amelaxa(Oksana Amelina)/DepositPhotos.com; page 89 © 2018 Palmiche Press; page 92 (math workstation) © 2013 Ashley Cross/mrscrossthirdgrade.blogspot.com; page 92 (wall poster) © 2018 Palmiche Press; page 93 (classroom) pixabay.com; page 93 (family watching TV) © 2013 DragonImages/DepositPhotos.com; page 96 © 2012 mtkang/DepositPhotos.com; page 97 © 2018 Palmiche Press; page 98 (visual discrimination) © 2018 Palmiche Press; page 98 (figure ground) © 2018 Pal-miche Press; page 98 (visual closure) © 2018 Palmiche Press; page 98 (birds) © 2018 Palmiche Press; page 100 © 2014 yusufdemirci/DepositPhotos.com; page 101 © 2013 DesignPicsInc/DepositPhotos.com; page 102 © 2013 imagesbykenny/DepositPhotos.com; page 104 © 2017 yacobchuk1/DepositPhotos.com; page 108 © 2018 Palmiche Press; page 112 (community service) © 2013 Michael Jung/DepositPhotos.com; page 112 (criminal justice) © 2017 zimmytws/DepositPhotos.com; page 128 © 2017 Educational Alternatives; page 150 © 2018 Palmiche Press

All rights reserved. Unless otherwise noted, no part of this book may be reproduced, stored in a retrieval system, or transmitted in any form or by any means, electronic, mechanical, photocopying, recording, or other-wise, without express written permission of the author, except for brief quotations or critical reviews. For more information, please write to Educational Alternatives, LLC at the address below.

Palmiche Press, Inc. is a registered trademark.

Published by Adam Sugerman, Palmiche Press, Inc.
Edited by Elan Elyachar-Stahl, Ruth Turner, and Adam Sugerman
Contributions from Ron Romanowicz and Bill Stern
Cover, interior design, illustrations, glossary, and index by Adam Sugerman

ISBN 978-0-9968467-0-7

10 9 8 7 6 5 4 3 2 1
Printed in Colombia by Panamericana Formas e Impresos S.A.

Educational Alternatives, LLC.
35 Lily Pond Lane
Katonah, NY 10536

The companion guide to *The ABCs of Learning Issues* for teachers is *BOXES*®.

The ABCs of Learning Issues and *BOXES* are also available in the Spanish language.

Educational Alternatives offers compassionate and professional educational consulting. Please contact Dana Stahl at danaconsults@gmail.com for pricing information on packages that include professional services and books.

Dedication

To my family who stood by my side through an emotionally challenging time and encouraged me to channel my energy in a positive direction. With their love and support I created Educational Alternatives, LLC. Today, my practice affords me the opportunity to provide educational advice, advocacy, and placement to an array of families. My husband and our children continue their unwavering support. They graciously remind me that there are many ways in which to find success.

Acknowledgements

The expression "the journey is the destination" describes my story: I went from being a child with learning disabilities to a learning specialist who understands children's strengths and vulnerabilities while simultaneously helping them develop compensatory strategies to achieve academic success.

There once was a time when the thought of writing a three-paragraph essay on a blank piece of paper was a terrifying experience. Writing *The ABCs of Learning Issues* and *BOXES* is the culmination of years of academic support, familial cheerleaders, and a great deal of personal perseverance.

This book would not be possible without the continued support of my mentor, Betty Osman, a well-known psychologist and author, who told me at age 11, "You are a very bright young girl who just needs a different way to learn." Betty provided hope and instilled a sense of academic self-confidence that carried me through my bachelor's degree at Boston University and my master's degree at the College of William and Mary.

Ruth Turner, my great aunt and former Director of Consumer Reports books, spent countless hours reviewing *BOXES* and encouraging me to keep taking the small steps needed in order to develop my practice, Educational Alternatives, LLC.

Elan Elyachar-Stahl, my daughter, an educator and licensed midwife, expanded the framework of *BOXES* and *The ABCs of Learning Issues* that enhanced the depth and clarity of the material presented.

Ron Romanowicz, a friend and former colleague, was the first person I worked with on *BOXES* in a professional capacity. Together, Ron and I presented to the faculty at The Harvey School in Katonah, New York profiles of students who had identified learning issues, the behaviors their teachers may observe in class, and effective teaching strategies educators could incorporate through differential instruction.

Adam Sugerman, a new friend, colleague, and publisher, worked tirelessly and patiently to update and edit the information in *BOXES*, to help develop *The ABCs of Learning Issues*, to translate my works into the Spanish language, and to provide technical assistance in their publication and dissemination.

I thank Betty, Ruth, Elan, Ron, and Adam for helping me to reach a place in life where I can share some of my experiences with educators and parents in my ongoing quest to help children reach their full potential.

Contents

A Note from the Author

I wrote this book to help parents understand the behaviors that their children with identified learning issues may experience in school and at home. Every industry has a specific language. The language of learning issues that educators use is specific to the world of teachers, educational administrators, child psychologists and psychiatrists, social workers, speech and language pathologists, pediatric neurologists, and occupational and physical therapists. Without understanding the precise terminology common to these professionals and to this industry, parents are at a disadvantage in grasping key components of specific clinical definitions, effective teaching strategies, and techniques they can incorporate at home to help them accept and support their children who experience learning issues.

The ABCs of Learning Issues will help parents and guardians further their understanding of various learning issues and behaviors that they observe in their home and hear about from their children's teachers. The information presented empowers parents to identify, recognize, and deal with specific learning issues that are described in formal evaluations, on standardized tests, and within school environments. This book also includes specific strategies and examples of clinical and educators' definitions to help parents understand what these definitions mean, recognize the significance of behaviors they may observe at home, and learn about effective strategies to incorporate at school and at home. There is also a list of professionals who can assist in treating specific learning issues and a section on educational topics and concerns that parents may have that are presented in a series of articles in a question-and-answer format, promoting a dialogue for future conversations.

As an educational diagnostician for more than thirty years, I work with families to help them to fully understand the results and interpretations of formal evaluations. I work with children on developing their academic skill set and preparing them for their next educational crossroad. With an in-depth background in learning disabilities, I provide a wide array of academic recommendations and interventions to parents and professionals. The clinical and educator's definitions and effective teaching strategies and home strategies presented in *The ABCs of Learning Issues* are based upon my personal experience as a learning specialist. Differential instruction is an umbrella term that is popular among educators today. However, all children benefit from differential instruction when incorporating a multi-modality approach in learning or when reinforcing concepts. Thus, the strategies presented in this book will help all children to reach their full social-emotional and academic potential.

The ABCs of Learning Issues provides parents with a valuable tool that increases their understanding of learning issues, offers a framework in which to identify and incorporate effective strategies when helping their children, and assists them in learning how to work directly with their school in a cooperative and collaborative manner.

How to Use
The ABCs of Learning Issues

There are a number of scenarios in which this book may help you and your child. The following situations are two examples:

SCENARIO 1

If you notice that your child acts in a way that you suspect demonstrates a learning issue, browse the index of this book until you see the identified behavior listed. Then consult the information provided pertaining to the behaviors identified in the corresponding learning issues to learn how best to support your child at home, as well as find professionals who can provide appropriate support and intervention. If your child is between the ages of three and 21, you will also find a sample letter to request help on page 130, and starting on page 78 an explanation of the process schools use to seek assistance for students.

Sample letter

Marta Smith
3333 Lakeside Drive
Katonah, NY 10536

Jose Marti Elementary School
578 North Main Street
Katonah, NY 10536

October 15, 2018

Dear Principal Jones,

I am writing to you today regarding my increased concern for my son, _____. He is experiencing challenges within the classroom and at home that to date are adversely affecting his academic performance. I am requesting that a complete psychoeducational evaluation be administered. It is my sincere hope that the findings provide us with educational strategies to help him feel more comfortable and confident in his classes.

Please let me know what I can do to help facilitate this process. I am available to discuss my concerns further at a team meeting where his teachers can share their observations and we can begin to understand the reasons he is struggling in school.

Sincerely,

Marta Smith

cc: name of classroom teacher
    name of the director of support services

Tips for composing the letter

When composing the letter, please note the following points:

- Sometimes parents' concerns are academic, behavioral, or attention related. State your concerns and describe your observations. Speak in the first person and remember that a successful path requires a partnership with your school. Remain positive and request what you want. After all, parents are their children's advocates.

- Once the school receives a written letter requesting that a psychoeducational evaluation be administered, the school has 30 days in which to start to carry out this request.

SCENARIO 2

Your child's teacher or other school support personnel member may notice an academic, social-emotional, or behavioral issue in school and will request a meeting with you. The information beginning on page 2 will allow you to learn about specific learning issues, a list of professionals that the school or you may be able to provide based upon individual needs, and recommended strategies in both the classroom and at home that will help to foster a skillset to compensate for identified learning issues. *The ABCs of Learning Issues* also provides information to help parents prepare for parent-teacher conferences, Committee for Preschool Special Education (CPSE) and Committee for Special Education (CSE) meetings starting on page 78.

Tour of The ABCs of Learning Issues

This color indicates the places in this book where this learning issue is applicable.

This page number is where the learning issue is explained in detail.

LEARNING ISSUES	1
■ Academic Anxiety with Regard to Performance	2
☐ Academic Anxiety with Regard to Transitions	6

Name of Learning Issue ——————————— **Executive Functioning Skills**

The definition of the learning issue ——————— Clinical definition
from the point of view of speech
and language pathologists, school Executive functions are a set of cognitive processes that are
psychologists, psychiatrists, nurses, and necessary for controlling one's own behavior in order to
other professionals outside the school. achieve a goal. Executive functions include basic cognitive
processes that involve a part of the brain called the frontal lobe.
This part of the brain helps people pay attention, manage their
time and their emotions. Executive functioning allows people
to make good decisions by either promoting or inhibiting
When applicable, the color tab connects certain behaviors. Higher order executive functions require the
this particular learning issue with a topic simultaneous use of multiple basic executive functions.
of education discussed in depth as well
as additional information your child's Educators' definition
teacher may have.
Executive functioning is a series of mental
skills that help the brain organize
and act on information. Executive
The definition of the learning issue ——————— functions are necessary for
from the point of view of teachers, people to pay attention, hold
academic tutors, coaches, school onto information, block out
principals, and other learning specialists irrelevant stimuli, organize and
prioritize information, and initiate tasks.

The definition of the learning issue from ——————— What do these definitions mean?
the point of view of a layperson
People who struggle with executive functions have difficulty
with the initiation and completion of tasks, solving complex
problems, and regulating their own behavior.

Behaviors children demonstrate ——————— Which behaviors may parents observe if
when they have a particular their child demonstrates this learning issue?
learning issue
• Your child might appear scattered, forgetful, and inattentive.
• Maintaining sustained attention is challenging.
• Time management and organization is close to non-existent.
• Your child might act before thinking through the consequences of
his behavior, and therefore he might get into trouble fairly often.

Whom to call?
What to do?
Where to go?

Types of professionals who can assist ——————— Which professionals can treat this
your child with this learning issue learning issue?
• Learning specialists
• Classroom teachers
• Parents

Which teaching strategies can be effective in school?

- Create a structured learning environment and approach assigned tasks with sequential steps that have a logical order.
- Provide students with an outline of the lesson.
- Use weekly planners that break assignments down into small tasks.
- Check in frequently with students to make sure they understand the work.

Which strategies can help at home?

- Time management and routines are essential.
- Use calendars to plan for weekly and long term assignments.
- Assist in the initiation of assignments. Offer support during the completion of tasks, and help your child assess for thoroughness and accuracy.
- Use tools like calendars, smartphone apps, and alarm clock reminders to help your child remember appointments, assignments, and planned activities.

For additional resources or if you have a question, ask Dana at **EducationalAlternativesLLC.com/educational-advice**

———— Helpful school strategies

———— Helpful home strategies

———— Ask Ms. Stahl a question

Topic discussed in depth

Tips for Children with Poor Executive Function Skills

What Tips Can You Offer Children with Poor Executive Function Skills?

Students who exhibit executive functioning challenges need to prioritize the most important steps required to complete assignments. They need to plan ahead, thinking about the steps necessary to organize their time, and estimating how much time each step may take to complete.

According to researchers at the Harvard's Center on the Developing Child, executive function allows us to manage ourselves and access our resources in order to achieve a specific task. It involves both mental control and self-regulation. The Center describes executive function and self-regulation skills as the mental processes that enable us to plan, focus attention, remember instructions, and juggle multiple tasks successfully. In their literature, they describe three types of brain function: working memory, mental flexibility, and self-control:

- Working memory allows us to retain and manipulate distinct pieces of information over short periods of time.

94   THE ABCS OF LEARNING ISSUES

- Mental flexibility helps us to sustain shifting our attention in response to different demands or to apply different rules in different settings.
- Self-control enables us to set priorities and resist impulsive actions or response.

Students with executive function challenges will benefit from organizing their materials before they start work on a project. With long-term assignments, students should initiate a plan in a timely fashion. During the interval between initiation and completion of a task, students need to complete multiple steps and use great diligence, which is often daunting and overwhelming. To succeed, students must be persistent and mindful of each section of a specific task with the strength to forge ahead as they complete interim steps along the way.

When students feel frustrated and experience performance anxiety, they may find it helpful to keep their cool by regulating their emotions and trying a 'smash the task' approach. Using this technique, students can break down assignments into manageable components. In this way, they lessen their angsts while demonstrating progress in completing assigned tasks. Students also benefit from the ability to think flexibly in their approach to an assignment so they can change their strategies when needed. Controlling impulsive reactions allows them

TOPICS IN EDUCATION   95

to think before they act and to keep distractions in check. By stopping, thinking and then acting, students are able to assess their options, which allows them to make sound decisions. Students need to learn how to transition from one task to another when they have completed one portion of an assigned task and need to initiate work on other parts.

Understanding how to navigate and negotiate assignments permits students to work efficiently and effectively from initiation to completion of tasks. By using some of the strategies described above, children will improve their executive function skills. Ultimately, this will enhance the likelihood that your children will complete assignments to the best of their ability.

Source: Executive Function & Self-Regulation, Center on the Developing Child at Harvard University

For additional resources or if you have a question, ask Dana at **EducationalAlternativesLLC.com/educational-advice**

96   THE ABCS OF LEARNING ISSUES

LEARNING ISSUES

Academic Anxiety with Regard to Performance

Clinical definition

Anxiety may be a normal part of life, and it can also be maladaptive if excessive feelings of fear, worry, or nervousness interfere with everyday life. Anxiety levels are linked to internal pressure that the students may place on themselves, as well as how they perceive their family members' and teachers' expectations, as well.

Educators' definition

Performance anxiety interferes with the learning process as students tend to shut down and cannot fully engage with the material presented in class due to fear or worry of underachieving.

What do these definitions mean?

Students have an inner fear that they aren't going to perform to the best of their ability so they freeze. Due to the anxiety, they underperform. It is as if they get stage fright when presented with assigned tasks. Academic anxiety with regard to performance may manifest as a gap between children's academic abilities and their academic performance.

Which behaviors may parents observe if their child demonstrates this learning issue?

- Children may demonstrate anxiety when initiating tasks.
- They may need ongoing guidance and positive reinforcement while preparing and completing assignments.
- They are fearful that they will not be able to complete or comprehend assigned tasks.
- They may be reluctant to attend school.

Which professionals can treat this learning issue?

- Child psychiatrists
- School psychologists
- Learning specialists
- Classroom teachers
- Academic tutors

Which teaching strategies can be effective in school?

- Create learning environments that encourage students to independently navigate and negotiate their academic work.
- Lower the overall level of uncertainty in the classroom by clearly stating the short- and long-term goals of learning.

- Allow students to monitor their own short- and long-term academic growth.
- Offer direct instruction to students before beginning independent assignments.
- Provide detailed outlines to study from and to refer to when completing assignments and preparing for tests.

Which strategies can help at home?

- Teach your child to "smash the task," or break it down into manageable components. Students develop a sense of ownership in accomplishing small segments of assignments, which lowers their anxiety and allows for successful completion.
- Provide ongoing support when your child is preparing and completing tasks.
- Create study guides and outlines that help your child prepare for quizzes and tests.
- Encourage your child to meditate. If you or your child does not have any prior experience with meditation, there are many websites and free podcasts that provide guided meditation for relaxation and focus. You can try it together!
- Remind your children to breathe deeply when they feel stressed.
- Spend time with your children and encourage them to discuss their concerns.

How to use a chime to teach children mindfulness...

The Sound Stopped

It Sounds Softer

It Sounds LOUD

When I pay attention to sound in a special way... it helps clear my mind and I feel calmer and more focused

Source: kristinamarcelli.wordpress.com

Children can incorporate mindfulness by stopping, redirecting, and replacing negative thoughts with positive experiences.

For additional resources or if you have a question, ask Dana at **EducationalAlternativesLLC.com/educational-advice**

Academic Anxiety with Regard to Transitions

Clinical definition

Anxiety may be a normal part of life, and it can also be maladaptive if excessive feelings of fear, worry, or nervousness interfere with everyday life. Anxiety levels are linked to internal pressure that the students may place on themselves, as well as how they perceive their family members' and teachers' expectations, as well.

Educators' definition

Settling into class and transitioning from one task to another can cause the student to feel anxious and uncertain, which can interrupt the learning process. Students may present as ill-prepared for class and appear unable to begin the class period.

What do these definitions mean?

When students complete an assignment and shift to another, they can become uneasy and have difficulty focusing on the new topic. This is especially apt to occur when clear expectations and routines are not in place. Students may feel a loss of control if they don't know what is coming next. These students need extra support to prepare for transitions.

Which behaviors may parents observe if their child demonstrates this learning issue?

- Children may feel anxious and uncertain when shifting between activities.
- Anxiety is lessened when routines remain consistent.

Which professionals can treat this learning issue?

- Child psychiatrists
- School psychologists
- Learning specialists
- Classroom teachers
- Academic tutors

Which teaching strategies can be effective in school?

- Review the schedule for the day or class period and point out anticipated transitions so students know what to expect.
- State clear expectations for class lessons and assignments.
- Make sure that directions are both verbally and visually presented.
- Display visual aids on the wall stating behavioral expectations during academic and recreational transitions.

Which strategies can help at home?

- Develop a consistent routine from the end of the school day to bedtime.

- Help your child transition from one activity or assignment to another by guiding them.

- Validate your children's experiences and empathize with their feelings.

 For additional resources or if you have a question, ask Dana at
EducationalAlternativesLLC.com/educational-advice

Attending to Academic Task

Clinical definition

Attending to academic tasks refers to a student's ability to connect to scholastic activities and maintain their focus and motivation on an intellectual, socio-emotional, behavioral, and physical level.

Educators' definition

Students lose focus and appear to daydream before they re-enter the discussion. They have difficulty transitioning from one part of the lesson to another. There is a visible disconnect from directions to execution of tasks.

What do these definitions mean?

Students lose track of where they are in the lesson being presented. Although they can appear to be paying attention, they are often in a daze and lose focus.

Which behaviors may parents observe if their child demonstrates this learning issue?

- Children may demonstrate anxiety when initiating tasks.

- They need sustained guidance with preparing and completing assignments.

- They lose track of the task at hand and space out.

Which professionals can treat this learning issue?

- Learning specialists

- Classroom teachers

- Academic tutors

Which teaching strategies can be effective in school?

- Incorporate visual, auditory, and kinesthetic clues to help students remain focused.

- Charts, maps, and graphs all aid in helping students keep track of where teachers are in the lesson.

- Physical proximity to the student as well as call-and-response techniques can help to refocus attention.

- Keep track of the time and the activity in which students lose focus. Do they lose focus at the same time each day? Do they always lose focus during a specific activity?

Which strategies can help at home?

- A workspace free of distractions. These distractions may include television, computer games, and telephones.
- Provide head sets to block out surrounding noise.
- Create a cubicle workspace to increase sustained attention.
- Supervise your children while they do their homework.
- Encourage breaks, allowing them to stretch and refocus.
- Give positive reinforcement and rewards for staying on task.

If your child appears to be distracted or avoids work and is displaying difficulty performing a certain type of activity, the work may be too difficult. Ask your child to rate the activity on a scale of 1 to 10 to assess if this is the case. If he says that the activity is a 7 or higher, simplify the activity through modeling or by working together.

For additional resources or if you have a question, ask Dana at **EducationalAlternativesLLC.com/educational-advice**

Auditory Integration

Clinical definition

Auditory integration is a process that usually occurs in the brain automatically when people make meaning out of the sounds, syllables, and words that they hear. A person who has difficulties with auditory integration struggles to understand the subtle differences in words and sounds, and therefore, they may not understand the meaning of what people say.

Educators' definition

Children who have auditory integration issues struggle to understand what is said even though they have normal hearing. Something occurs in the brain while processing sounds that jumbles the words, and the child cannot make sense of the information.

What do these definitions mean?

This means that while these students may hear the information presented in class, they do not understand auditory information (information obtained by listening) in the same way as other children. This could affect many other areas of learning in the classroom since a lot of information is shared orally.

Which behaviors may parents observe if their child demonstrates this learning issue?

• When giving directions, your child's responses might be delayed.

• Your child's reactions or responses to verbal information may seem off topic.

• If you give directions with multiple steps, they might follow through with only the first or second task.

• Detailed stories are not fully understood. Your child picks up on parts of the story and misses important details. For example, if you said, "The red bird sat on the green roof," your child might process, "The bird is on the roof."

Which professionals can treat this learning issue?

• Speech and language pathologists

• Learning specialists

• Classroom teachers

Which teaching strategies can be effective in school?

• Teach in a multisensory fashion using visual aids that reinforce specific concepts presented in class so that students do not need to rely solely on auditory cues.

- Movies, videos, photographs, diagrams, graphs, and charts can help illustrate orally presented concepts.

- Create class notes and outlines to help students obtain the information presented in class. This will help them at home when they have to do their work independently.

Which strategies can help at home?

- Provide homework support with visual aids such as illustrated examples, pictures, graphs, maps, and charts along with manipulatives like dice, rulers, and calculators to assist in understanding information that was presented verbally.

- Watch movies that coincide with assigned literature. For example, when reading *To Kill a Mockingbird*, watch the movie and ask questions to help your child think critically, predict outcomes, and compare and contrast.

Auditory integration is sometimes improved by incorporating other senses when attempting to process information. To ensure that your children have understood what they have heard, ask them to repeat or summarize what you have said.

For additional resources or if you have a question, ask Dana at **EducationalAlternativesLLC.com/educational-advice**

Auditory Working Memory and Retrieval

Clinical definition

Auditory Working Memory (AWM) is the process of actively keeping sounds in mind for short periods of time when the sounds are no longer in the environment. Retrieval is the process of calling that information to mind when it's needed. AWM along with retrieval refer to a cerebral system that temporarily stores and manages information that people need to perform complex cognitive tasks such as learning, reasoning, and comprehension.

When students have issues with AWM and retrieval, their ability to recall newly acquired information is affected. While some memories are long-term, auditory working memories last just a few seconds; making these very short-term memories and recalling them are essential for everyday learning.

> **Vocabulary**
>
> Long-term Memory: A vast store of knowledge and recall of information over a long period of time.
>
> Short-term Memory: The mind's ability to recall information for a limited period of time.
>
> Working Memory: Short-term memory used to carry out interim steps to process information.

Educators' definition

Auditory working memory and retrieval describes the process of receiving and holding onto auditory information in an area of the brain that controls short-term memories. When students struggle with AWM and retrieval, it means they struggle to make very short-term memories of sounds recently heard, hold onto the sounds, and recall them when necessary.

What do these definitions mean?

Students have difficulty remembering the information they just heard. Although they may listen attentively, it is as if the information goes in one ear and out the other. Their long-term memory appears normal, whereas their auditory short-term memory may seem impaired.

As a result of this learning issue, students have difficulty when information is presented orally both at home and at school. Since these students have trouble retaining auditory information in the short term, they also struggle to produce meaningful information about something they just heard.

Utilizing additional senses such as sight and touch can enhance auditory working memory and retrieval.

Which behaviors may parents observe if their child demonstrates this learning issue?

• Your child struggles to remember information that they hear.

• If your child receives too much auditory information at one time, they seem unable to take in that information and remember it.

• When carrying out instructions, your child loses track of the details.

• Children appear to listen very carefully with their eyes focused on you, but they often do not absorb or make sense of what they hear. They may remember a word or two, or part of a thought, but do not demonstrate a deeper understanding.

Which professionals can treat this learning issue?

• Speech and language therapists

• Learning specialists

Which teaching strategies can be effective in school?

• Note-taking strategies and visual graphic organizers will assist students in adapting to a higher level of language processing.

• Incorporate student-led group discussions.

- Use media to bring class content to life. Examples include *The History Channel*, *The Discovery Channel*, and multimedia alternatives such as educational websites.
- Allow additional time to copy from the board.

Which strategies can help at home?

- Use visual aids.
- Create outlines, vocabulary lists, and definitions.
- Highlight sections of the text that reinforce information being discussed in class.
- Create flash cards to highlight important information and to refer back to each subject.
- To demonstrate total comprehension, encourage retelling stories with the main idea and supporting details.
- All the above suggestions can be incorporated into teaching and tutoring practices.

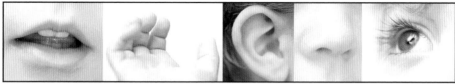

Use additional senses to enhance meaning and recall of newly acquired information.

For additional resources or if you have a question, ask Dana at **EducationalAlternativesLLC.com/educational-advice**

Computational Accuracy

Clinical definition

Computational accuracy is the ability to calculate a mathematical equation and arrive at the correct numerical value. Students who struggle with computational accuracy may lack the ability to accurately perform simple math calculations despite possessing a conceptual understanding of numbers and mathematical concepts.

Educators' definition

Students who experience difficulty with computational accuracy struggle to correctly compute simple math facts although they may have a deeper conceptual understanding of mathematical operations and numerical relationships. Although students display effort to compute correctly, they arrive at incorrect answers for other reasons.

To help facilitate computational accuracy, have children use their fingers, computational tables, rulers, calculators, and any tool they need to help accuracy once they have an understanding of the concept behind the computation.

What do these definitions mean?

Students are not able to manipulate number facts in their head. They miscalculate basic number facts relating to addition, subtraction, multiplication, and division, and do not develop automaticity, which is the ability to know a number fact like the back of your hand.

Vocabulary

Basic Number Facts: Automaticity of the computation of numbers from 0 through 10 in addition, subtraction, multiplication, and division. Students need to master and to recall them instantly.

Which behaviors may parents observe if their child demonstrates this learning issue?

• Your child struggles to calculate simple math problems.

• When setting up handwritten math problems, your child misaligns the rows of numbers, and therefore calculates the math problem incorrectly.

• Children can understand math concepts, but are unable to calculate the correct answer.

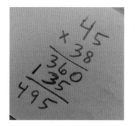

Misaligning numbers may cause incorrect answers. In the image on the left, the temporary ones digit "5" in 135 should be aligned under the tens digit "6" in 360.

By utilizing large boxed graph paper as in the image on the right, children can properly place and align numbers in the correct place value position.

Which professionals can treat this learning issue?

- Learning specialists
- Classroom teachers
- Parents

Which teaching strategies can be effective in school?

- Provide a visual point of reference of math facts, percentages, decimals and fractions, conversion tables for the metric and U.S. customary systems.
- Supply these students with calculators and ensure that they know how to utilize them efficiently and effectively when performing their school assignments.

Which strategies can help at home?

- Provide calculators, rulers, measuring cups, and conversion charts to assist in calculating answers.
- Practice addition and multiplication facts.
- Practice percentages, decimals, fractions, and metric conversions.
- For two-digit numbers or larger, use graph paper to help your children align numbers correctly.

 For additional resources or if you have a question, ask Dana at **EducationalAlternativesLLC.com/educational-advice**

Decoding Skills

Clinical definition

Decoding is the practice of using various reading skills to translate written words on a page into sounds that are read aloud. When readers decode, they sound out words by pronouncing their parts and then joining those parts together to form cohesive words.

Educators' definition

Students who struggle with decoding have difficulty sounding out unfamiliar words and reading with expression. Reading rate, accuracy, and fluency are often underdeveloped.

What do these definitions mean?

People with decoding issues are usually avoidant readers who struggle with sounding words out, reading out loud with accuracy and reading with expression. Reading comprehension is often comprised due to gaps in accuracy and fluency.

Reading with a partner facilitates and fosters comfort and familiarity with new words.

Which behaviors may parents observe if their child demonstrates this learning issue?

- Children are unable to sound out unfamiliar words.

- They struggle with syllabication rules.

- The reading rate is extremely slow.

- Reading accuracy is reduced through omissions, additions, and mispronunciations of words.

Which professionals can treat this learning issue?

- Speech and language therapist
- Learning specialist

Which teaching strategies can be effective in school?

- Avoid round robin approach to reading novels.

- Allow students to raise their hand and volunteer when the class is reading out loud. Do not call upon a student who is unprepared to read out loud.

- Allow students to prepare ahead of time by telling them in advance that they will be responsible to read a particular section.

Which strategies can help at home?

- Take turns reading with your child.
- Exaggerate reading with expression to facilitate varying voices for different characters.
- Read comic books, magazines, and plays to increase decoding skills and reading rate and to practice out loud with expression.
- Listen to books on tape while simultaneously reading the book.

Tapping out and counting syllables is an effective compensatory strategy to use when learning to read.

For additional resources or if you have a question, ask Dana at
EducationalAlternativesLLC.com/educational-advice

Executive Functioning Skills

Clinical definition

Executive functions are a set of cognitive processes that are necessary for controlling one's own behavior in order to achieve a goal. Executive functions include basic cognitive processes that involve a part of the brain called the *frontal lobe*. This part of the brain helps people pay attention, manage their time and their emotions. Executive functioning allows people to make good decisions by either promoting or inhibiting certain behaviors. Higher order executive functions require the simultaneous use of multiple basic executive functions.

Educators' definition

Executive functioning is a series of mental skills that help the brain organize and act on information. Executive functions are necessary for people to pay attention, hold onto information, block out irrelevant stimuli, organize and prioritize information, and initiate tasks.

What do these definitions mean?

People who struggle with executive functions have difficulty with the initiation and completion of tasks, solving complex problems, and regulating their own behavior.

Which behaviors may parents observe if their child demonstrates this learning issue?

- Your child might appear scattered, forgetful, and inattentive.
- Maintaining sustained attention is challenging.
- Time management and organization is close to non-existent.
- Your child might act before thinking through the consequences of his behavior, and therefore he might get into trouble fairly often.

Whom to call?
What to do?
Where to go?

Which professionals can treat this learning issue?

- Learning specialists
- Classroom teachers
- Parents

Which teaching strategies can be effective in school?

- Create a structured learning environment and approach assigned tasks with sequential steps that have a logical order.
- Provide students with an outline of the lesson.
- Use weekly planners that break assignments down into small tasks.
- Check in frequently with students to make sure they understand the work.

Which strategies can help at home?

- Time management and routines are essential.
- Use calendars to plan for weekly and long term assignments.
- Assist in the initiation of assignments. Offer support during the completion of tasks, and help your child assess for thoroughness and accuracy.
- Use tools like calendars, smartphone apps, and alarm clock reminders to help your child remember appointments, assignments, and planned activities.

 For additional resources or if you have a question, ask Dana at
EducationalAlternativesLLC.com/educational-advice

Expressive Language

Clinical definition

Expressive language is defined as the "output" of language, or what a person puts out into the world in order to communicate their wishes and needs. The term expressive language includes verbal language, written language, and nonverbal body language.

Educators' definition

Expressive language involves the use of speech, writing, and non-verbal communication, like facial expressions and gestures, to convey a message to others. People with expressive language difficulties struggle to respond to other people by using verbal communication, written communication and/or body language, despite having intact receptive language capabilities.

What do these definitions mean?

Expressive language issues adversely impact people's ability to communicate their thoughts and ideas. While people with expressive language issues understand what is said to them (receptive language), they struggle with verbalizing, writing and/or physically expressing their thoughts and ideas (expressive language).

Which behaviors may parents observe if their child demonstrates this learning issue?

- Your child will answer direct questions with one- or two-word answers.
- They will rarely elaborate on an idea or provide a detailed account of their experiences.
- Their choice of vocabulary is limited and unsophisticated.
- Written expression may be tedious and result in an underdeveloped written product.
- Your child's body language might not correspond with how they feel about a certain situation.

Which professionals can treat this learning issue?

- Speech and language therapists
- Learning specialists
- Classroom teachers
- Parents

Which teaching strategies can be effective in school?

- Promote active participation in class discussions and on pen-and-paper activities.

- Include the use of visual aids to increase students' use of content-based vocabulary.

- Visual graphic organizers assist in developing expressive language production.

- Use sentence expanders to enhance written expression.

Which strategies can help at home?

- Use who, what, when, why, where, and how questions when talking with your child. Avoid yes-and-no questions.

- Use sentence expanders to enhance written expression that include who, what, when, where, why and how responses. For example, *The boy ran* is a sentence, but it does not elicit a lot of information. Help your child expand the sentence by asking questions such as: *How did the boy run? Where did the boy run?*

- Show your child how the answers to these questions changes the sentence to *The boy ran very fast in the park.*

Describing how you feel using descriptors such as who, what, when, where, and why promotes expressive language.

For additional resources or if you have a question, ask Dana at **EducationalAlternativesLLC.com/educational-advice**

Immature Social Judgment

Clinical definition

Some children and adolescents engage in social behavior typical of younger children. This can occur for several reasons. One possible reason is that children's general development is below that of their peers. If so, immature behavior might be expected in other areas of development, not only in social relations. Either way, it is possible and imperative to help children improve their social and relational skills.

Educators' definition

Immature social judgment interferes with a child's ability to make sound social decisions and can affect their ability to maintain lasting friends. These children are on the periphery within their school community.

What do these definitions mean?

Age-appropriate social interactions with peers are underdeveloped and are often disruptive. Students are not able to pick up on verbal and nonverbal social cues.

Which behaviors may parents observe if their child demonstrates this learning issue?

- Your child seeks the friendship of younger children.

- They are more comfortable following the crowd and do not seek out leadership opportunities.

- They often find themselves in trouble.

- They cannot pick up on social cues.

- They often hang with friends who are not truly friends.

Which professionals can treat this learning issue?

- Child psychologists

- School psychologists

- Licensed clinical social workers

Which teaching strategies can be effective in school?

- Teach students about appropriate and inappropriate peer-to-peer interactions.

- Encourage students to reflect on their own behavior, including when they exhibit model behavior.

- Seek out opportunities to analyze characters' behaviors and decision-making processes in the texts you read as a class.
- Connect the student to resources that provide structured social time, such as clubs and activity groups.

Which strategies can help at home?

- Arrange and monitor playdates.
- Participate in a local social skills group.
- Set rules and boundaries for appropriate and inappropriate behavior.
- At restaurants, play the game, "I Spy," and find people that depict different moods and social relationships, thus helping your child to notice body language and social cues.

DEVELOPING
MINDS

TABLE OF CONTENTS

1. HOW TO HELP KIDS FEEL CA
AND COPE WITH LIFE
2. KIDS GETTING ORGANIZED
MOTIVATED
3. KIDS CAN RESIST DISTRAC
TERM GOALS

Role playing helps to improve social judgment by rehearsing what to do and say in tenuous situations.

For additional resources or if you have a question, ask Dana at
EducationalAlternativesLLC.com/educational-advice

Immature Social-Emotional Development

Clinical definition

Social-emotional development refers to a person's ability to identify and understand their own feelings, manage their emotions, and self-regulate their behavior in a manner that is developmentally appropriate. Social-emotional development also includes a person's ability to assess and understand accurately the emotional states of others, to develop empathy for other people and living beings, and to establish and maintain relationships. Immature social-emotional development is evident when social-emotional skills appear to be underdeveloped, and therefore, the child does not behave at the expected level for their age.

Educators' definition

Immature social-emotional development interferes with a child's ability to develop age appropriate relationships with peers and adults. Their struggle to manage and regulate their emotions and behaviors limits their ability to socially or emotionally adapt to environmental situations during structured or unstructured time.

What do these definitions mean?

A child that has immature social-emotional development will struggle to form relationships with peers and elders, work collaboratively in groups, and extend empathy to others. They will likely exhibit a limited capacity to accept constructive criticism, make compromises, and accept other people's perspectives.

What behaviors may parents observe if their child demonstrates this learning issue?

• Your child may have low self-esteem.

• They often seek out the friendship of younger children.

• Their play and interests are not compatible with their peers.

• They tend to enjoy being on their own rather than in a group.

Which professionals can treat this learning issue?

• Child psychologists

• School psychologists

• Licensed clinical social workers

• Parents

Which teaching strategies can be effective in school?

- Develop students' sense of self-esteem by increasing their confidence as individuals and as learners.
- Create cooperative learning situations that lead to positive group interactions and opportunities for social and cognitive growth.

- Keep in close contact with students' advisors to apprise them of your observations.

Which strategies can help at home?

- Arrange and monitor playdates.
- Participate in a local social skills group.
- Facilitate playing on school and community sports teams, or joining after-school clubs.
- Model constructive criticism in your home and teach your child that it's okay to learn from each other's mistakes.

For additional resources or if you have a question, ask Dana at **EducationalAlternativesLLC.com/educational-advice**

Information Overload

Clinical definition

Information overload is a term used to describe a person who struggles to understand information and effectively utilize it to guide learning and decision-making processes when one receives too much information at a time.

Educators' definition

Students struggle to understand the content of the material presented because the volume of information presented is overwhelming to a student who struggles with information overload. All students feel overwhelmed by class content at some point, but students who struggle with information overload are frequently overwhelmed by content that other students can digest in a given class period.

What do these definitions mean?

A student that struggles with information overload will often underperform due to receiving too much information at one time. The sheer volume of content received is temporarily overwhelming. It is as if a circuit breaker shuts down.

Which behaviors may parents observe if their child demonstrates this learning issue?

• Your child may appear to be dazed or lost in thought.

• They reach their breaking point where they are no longer productive faster than you would expect for the task at hand.

Which professionals can treat this learning issue?

• Learning specialists

• Classroom teachers

Which teaching strategies can be effective in school?

• Present small chunks of information to students.

• Try to reduce the amount of information being presented in one class period.

Which strategies can help at home?

• Design a homework routine with frequent planned breaks.

• Break down assignments into manageable components.

• Communicate with professionals the level of information overload experienced at home.

 For additional resources or if you have a question, ask Dana at **EducationalAlternativesLLC.com/educational-advice**

Listening Comprehension

Clinical definition

Listening comprehension is a process that occurs in the brain that allows a person to understand and make meaning of spoken language. In order to understand spoken language, a person must understand phonemes (the basic sounds of a language), words (the vocabulary of a language), and the grammatical syntax of sentences (the structure of a language).

Educators' definition

Listening comprehension is more than just hearing what is said; it refers to children's capacity to understand sounds, words, and sentences, and to their ability to make meaning out of the messages they hear.

What do these definitions mean?

Students who have difficulty with listening comprehension struggle to remain connected during class discussions and lessons that cater to auditory learners because they are less able to keep up with the auditory information presented. Processing and assimilating auditory information is challenging for these students, as well as filtering out irrelevant auditory information.

Which behaviors may parents observe if their child demonstrates this learning issue?

• Your child answers direct questions with one- or two-word answers, and may seem unsure of what's been asked.

• They will miss the details of a story, and/or not understand a joke.

• They will be unable to follow conversations or make deeper connections.

Which professionals can treat this learning issue?

• Speech and language therapists

• Learning specialists

Which teaching strategies can be effective in school?

• Teach in a multi-sensory fashion using visual models that reinforce specific concepts being presented.

• Offer class notes and outlines to assure that students have the information being presented.

• Ask students to verbally repeat the directions prior to beginning their assigned tasks.

Which strategies can help at home?

- Limit background noise and auditory distractions when giving your child directions.

- Have important conversations in quiet environments.

- Simplify and shorten instructions. Start with a one-step direction and see how the child does, then continue with two-step directions, and so on.

- Ask questions during and after conversations to check for understanding.

- Listen to books on tape or audiobooks to increase listening skills.

- Read books to your children and tell them oral stories.

- Watch television programs together and ask questions to check for understanding.

- Be patient. Many parents believe their children are trying to defy them when the problem is they simply don't understand the message of what is being communicated.

For additional resources or if you have a question, ask Dana at
EducationalAlternativesLLC.com/educational-advice

Mathematical Conceptual Understanding

Clinical definition

Mathematical conceptual understanding is more than memorizing math facts and knowing how to calculate equations. Students with strong mathematical conceptual understanding have the ability to transfer their mathematical knowledge from one situation to another and apply known mathematical concepts in new contexts.

Educators' definition

Computational executions of basic math calculations are intact, but students lack the conceptual understanding of what is being presented.

What do these definitions mean?

Reduced conceptual understanding in math occurs when students do not understand why certain operations are performed in certain situations, and therefore, these students struggle to figure out which operation should be selected and used during the problem solving process.

Which behaviors may parents observe if their child demonstrates this learning issue?

- Your child is capable of completing math exercises and worksheets accurately without understanding the concepts behind their answers.
- They can accurately arrive at the correct answer without understanding the process. For example, they can add fractions without understanding what the fractions represent, or they can accurately compute 50 times 100 without understanding place values.

Which professionals can treat this learning issue?

- Learning specialists
- Math tutors
- Classroom teachers

Which teaching strategies can be effective in school?

- Use manipulatives to bridge an understanding between the abstract and the concrete.
- Using a hands-on approach can help close the gap between mathematical reasoning, problem-solving, and accurate execution.
- Use concrete examples to make strong connections.

Which strategies can help at home?

- Create fun learning experiences where fractions can be taught when eating pie, cake, or pizza.
- Bake cakes and teach dry and wet measurements in ounces, cups, pints, and quarts.
- Place meaning behind decimals, percentages, and fractions.
- Encourage real life applications at gas stations, such as estimating how many gallons to the mile as well as calculating change and tips.

Real-life math applications create teachable moments that foster conceptual understanding.

For additional resources or if you have a question, ask Dana at
EducationalAlternativesLLC.com/educational-advice

Organization and Time Management

Clinical definition

Organization and time management is the process of planning and exercising conscious control over the amount of time spent on specific activities, especially to increase efficacy, efficiency, or productivity.

Educators' definition

Students have difficulty planning, initiating, and completing assigned tasks in an organized and time efficient manner. They lack the ability to define and determine preplanning stages of executing tasks, including estimating the length of time an assigned task may require to complete.

What do these definitions mean?

Students who have issues with organization and time management struggle to organize notes, papers and files in a logical manner, and they often cannot accurately estimate how much time an assignment will take to complete. It is challenging for them to negotiate schoolwork independently.

Which behaviors may parents observe if their child demonstrates this learning issue?

- Their notebooks, binders, and backpacks are stuffed with papers and lack any semblance of organization.
- They do not remove old papers, quizzes, and tests from their binders.
- Papers for one subject are mixed with papers from another subject in their folders and binders.
- Essential papers may be missing or not securely positioned in safe and prominent places.
- Estimation of time to complete assignments is not close to accurate.
- Your child requires assistance with initiating assignments and navigating their way through them. Without this kind of help, tasks may not be completed at all.

Which professionals can treat this learning issue?

- Learning specialists
- Classroom teachers
- Academic tutors

Which teaching strategies can be effective in school?

- Have students color-code their binders, notebooks, and folders so that each color corresponds to a different subject.
- Check to see that they have the necessary notes and handouts to complete their assignments.
- Draft a schedule of assignments, breaking down specific due dates for each part of the assignment, rather than using one due date for the final product.
- Meet with students regularly to confirm that their agendas are up to date.
- Provide study skill strategies.

```
              Assignment: Persuasion Paper

Due Date: May 15                      Checklist of Things to Do for Step 1

Total Estimated Time Needed: 2 months      ☐   Read the newspaper.

Steps Involved
Step 1: Select a topic.                    ☐   Watch the TV news.
Step 2: Research your topic.
Step 3: Develop a thesis statement.
Step 4: Organize your materials.           ☐   Listen to programs on the radio.
Step 5: Write a rough draft.
Step 6: Organize your Works Cited page.
Step 7: Proofread and correct.             ☐   Download and listen to podcasts.
Step 8: Check information against sources.
Step 9: Incorporate final comments.
                                           ☐   Ask experts in your community.
Step 1: Select a topic.
Step 1 Deadline: February 21
```

Breaking tasks down into manageable components allows students to complete successfully specific sub-steps of long-term assignments.

Which strategies can help at home?

- Parents can assist their child to clean out and organize binders, folders, and backpacks on a weekly basis.
- Parents can assist their child to create folders for each subject, keeping quizzes, tests, and study guides for future reference in a safe place at home.
- Upon review of assigned tasks, parents can help their children estimate how much time it takes to complete a certain kind of assignment, and together they can assess whether their estimation was accurate.
- As needed, parents can assist their children to begin assignments and check in on them to help keep them focused and on-track.

Timed activities may cause some children to be stressed and anxious, preventing them from adequately completing assigned tasks.

 For additional resources or if you have a question, ask Dana at
EducationalAlternativesLLC.com/educational-advice

Processing Speed

Clinical definition

Processing speed is the rate at which the brain can absorb information, digest it, and create an appropriate response. Children who have reduced processing speed may produce the correct response at a slower rate than other children.

Educators' definition

When students with processing speed difficulties take in information, their brain requires more time to make sense of the information and task at hand, and it also takes them more time to produce their responses.

Children with reduced processing speed require additional time to digest and respond to information being presented.

What do these definitions mean?

Children process information slowly, reducing their ability to work efficiently and effectively within a specified time frame.

Which behaviors may parents observe if their child demonstrates this learning issue?

- Your child exhibits reduced performance when asked to complete tasks in a short amount of time. They can complete tasks, but struggle to do it under the pressure of a specific timeframe.
- Completion of assigned tasks takes an inordinate amount of time even though focus and effort is evident.

Which professionals can treat this learning issue?

- Learning specialists
- Classroom teachers
- Academic tutors

Which teaching strategies can be effective in school?

- Offer extended time and reduce the length of assignments.
- Reduce five paragraph essays to three, and ask for only odd or even numbers to be completed on assigned tasks.

- "Smash the task" down into manageable components and assign credit for each section.

Which strategies can help at home?

- Provide a calendar and create a schedule to help plan and complete long-term assignments.
- Break the assignment down into manageable components working toward completion.
- Share reading passages, brainstorm ideas for written responses, and proofread reports together.
- Model time-efficient and effective strategies.
- When assignments take too long and completion is unlikely, write a note to the teacher explaining the effort and obstacles that you observed. Respectfully request extra time. Older students can self-advocate and explain their difficulty.
- Take frequent planned breaks so your child can regroup and refocus their attention.

The speed at which children process information varies. Some children require more time to make sense of what they hear and to generate their responses.

For additional resources or if you have a question, ask Dana at
EducationalAlternativesLLC.com/educational-advice

Reading Comprehension

Clinical definition

Reading comprehension is the ability to read text, process it, and understand its meaning. An individual's ability to comprehend text is influenced by many different skills. Foundational reading skills, such as a person's ability to sight read (instantly recognize words on the page), decode unfamiliar words (sound out unknown words), and understand syntax (the structure of a sentence), affect a person's ability to engage with the higher-order reading skills, such as contemplating the deeper meaning of the text.

Educators' definition

Reading comprehension refers to a process that occurs when students can read, understand, and interpret written information. A student with reading comprehension issues struggles to make meaning out of the material that they read. It is challenging for these students to analyze the text at hand and make meaningful interpretations. Students may also struggle to correctly follow written directions.

What do these definitions mean?

Reading comprehension is understanding written language. When students struggle with reading comprehension, it is important that educators and parents alike investigate which foundational reading skills require strengthening. Identifying the area(s) of vulnerability to sight word vocabulary, decoding capabilities, or acquisition of information is essential in order to increase and ensure students' development of reading comprehension.

Which behaviors may parents observe if their child demonstrates this learning issue?

- These children can appear to read well but do not appear to grasp the meaning of what they read.
- Comprehension is compromised as a consequence of not being able to interpret and analyze reading material.

Which professionals can treat this learning issue?

- Reading specialists
- Learning specialists
- Academic tutors
- Classroom teachers

Which teaching strategies can be effective in school?

- Provide scaffolding so students can check their understanding as they go along. Every subject, whether it's math, science or language arts, requires strong scaffolding to support reading comprehension.
- Ask for written and/or verbal analysis in order to gauge your students' comprehension level.

Which strategies can help at home?

- Listen to books on tape or audiobooks while simultaneously reading the assigned text.
- Read with your child and ask for clarification about plot development, themes, character analysis, and making predictions.
- Highlight quotes and important passages in another color. This way, when you refer back to the book, the important sections will be easy to identify.
- Create a story map with characters, plots, and quotes to foster and facilitate comprehension.

 For additional resources or if you have a question, ask Dana at **EducationalAlternativesLLC.com/educational-advice**

Reading Rate

Clinical definition

Reading rate is the speed at which a person reads a written text during a specific unit of time. It is generally calculated by the number of words read per minute, but is influenced by a number of factors, such as a reader's purpose, level of expertise, and the relative difficulty of the text.

Educators' definition

Students who have a reduced reading rate accurately read and comprehend the material, but the pace at which they read is slower than expected due to reduced automaticity in being able to read words without hesitation and with appropriate expression. Reading rate increases with sound word recognition, a secure understanding of the subject matter, and the ability to decipher the text, puncutation, and purpose of the passage.

What do these definitions mean?

With a slow reading rate, keeping pace with one's peers is compromised. As content-based material is presented and the demands of reading increase, these students are at risk for not being able to keep up with the content of the curriculum.

Reading with fluency and expression is also harder to achieve for these students.

Which behaviors may parents observe if their child demonstrates this learning issue?

- Your child reads word-by-word instead of being able to group words and phrases together in meaningful chunks.
- They rarely read with any type of expressive voice.
- They lack confidence and are hesitant when sounding out unfamiliar words, reducing their accuracy in oral expression.
- Fluency is compromised by reduced accuracy, automaticity, and intonation.
- Your child appears to be more relaxed and reads at an increased rate when reading silently.

Which professionals can treat this learning issue?

- Reading specialists
- Learning specialists

Which teaching strategies can be effective in school?

- Teach students how to skim information on a page, and help students to implement skimming techniques effectively.

- Utilize visual graphic organizers that help define content-based material.
- Recommend books on tapes or audiobooks for assigned texts.
- Highlight quotes and important sections to aid in review of content material.
- Select reading material that is easy in order to focus on developing automaticity, appropriate phrasing, and intonation.

Which strategies can help at home?

- Use books on tape or audiobooks while simultaneously reading the book.
- Partner with your child to read books, magazines, and plays. Each take one or two characters and increase reading rate and expression with short passages.
- Help your child to skim and chunk text.
- Read material with your child that is below their reading level and in an area of interest to develop automaticity and to increase reading rate.
- Expand your child's vocabulary and increase their reading rate by fostering familiarity with the text.

For additional resources or if you have a question, ask Dana at
EducationalAlternativesLLC.com/educational-advice

Receptive Language

Clinical definition

Receptive language refers to a person's ability to understand language "input," which is the linguistic information a person receives from people and texts in their environment. Receptive language allows a person to understand the information they receive from other people's use of verbal, nonverbal, and written language. It also refers to a person's ability to make interpretations based on the language information they receive.

Educators' definition

Students who struggle with receptive language comprehension may find it challenging to understand and interpret auditory information, written information, and/or nonverbal information that they receive from people's body language. Although their expressive language may be intact ("output"), it might be difficult for them to produce the appropriate response based on a lack of comprehension of the "input."

What do these definitions mean?

People with receptive language issues may have difficulty understanding what is being said to them, what they are reading, or the gestures and facial expressions of those around them. They might understand the literal interpretation of the linguistic input, but struggle to understand subtleties and figurative significances.

Which behaviors may parents observe if their child demonstrates this learning issue?

- Your child may not follow directions well.
- They might not seem engaged in conversation, or their responses might seem a little off topic.
- Parents may need to repeat saying the same thing more than once.
- They may have difficulty answering direct or indirect questions.

Which professionals can treat this learning issue?

- Speech and language pathologists
- Learning specialists

Which teaching strategies can be effective in school?

- Design lessons that will develop visual problem-solving skills and mental manipulation of information in an attempt to bring words and images to life.

- Incorporate maps, charts, graphs, and real applications into your lessons to make necessary connections.

Which strategies can help at home?

- Limit background noise and auditory distractions when giving your child directions.

- Have important conversations in quiet environments.

- Simplify and shorten instructions. Start with a one-step direction and see how the child does, then continue with two-step directions, and so on.

- Be patient. Many parents believe their children are trying to defy them when the problem is they simply don't understand the message of what is being communicated.

For additional resources or if you have a question, ask Dana at
EducationalAlternativesLLC.com/educational-advice

Rote Memorization

Clinical definition

Rote memorization refers to a learning technique that is based on repetition. The basic concept is that the more a person repeats a concept, the more they are able to commit the concept to memory.

Educators' definition

Rote memorization refers to a learning process that requires students to memorize information by repeating. Students may not understand the concepts behind the facts they learn using this process. When students struggle with rote memorization, they struggle to memorize certain facts that other students internalize and commit to memory.

What do these definitions mean?

The information educators expect students to learn by rote memorization is information that, once memorized, essentially frees up the brain to focus on more conceptual tasks of learning. Basic math facts, spelling patterns, and vocabulary words are examples of information that often requires memorization.

Depending on the grade level of the student, specific facts and patterns of information are expected to be ready at hand in the child's brain. With rote memorization difficulties, the student has trouble committing these facts to memory, and therefore, they also struggle to recall basic information quickly when it is needed.

Which behaviors may parents observe if their child demonstrates this learning issue?

• Learning weekly spelling words, the alphabet, grammar rules, the number system, and basic math facts is difficult and unsuccessful.

• Your child cannot memorize facts just by repeating them, but is capable of knowing information that is acquired through other kinds of learning experiences.

Which professionals can treat this learning issue?

• Learning specialists

• Classroom teachers

Rote memorizaion becomes more useful when conceptual understanding accompanies the item to be learned.

Which teaching strategies can be effective in school?

- Provide students with multiplication and division fact sheets, and decimal conversions.
- Create lists of common spelling and vocabulary words for topics being covered in all content areas.
- Incorporate meaningful learning, associative learning, and active learning into lesson plans.
- Supply these students with calculators, Franklin Spellers®, tablets, and laptops.

Which strategies can help at home?

- Use visual aids that allow your child to fact check themselves, such as addition, subtraction, multiplication, and division fact tables.
- Display math problems in tandem with corresponding answers.
- Color code math facts with corresponding answers.
- Display vocabulary words in tandem with definitions.
- Color code vocabulary words with corresponding definitions.
- Create games that require your child to match vocabulary words with definitions, spelling words with spelling patterns, and math problems with their corresponding answers.

 For additional resources or if you have a question, ask Dana at
EducationalAlternativesLLC.com/educational-advice

Singular Approach to Learning

Clinical definition

Students that have a singular approach to learning concentrate very deeply on a single component of a single task. If they are asked to concentrate on more than one component of a single task, their ability to perform the task accurately is greatly diminished.

Educators' definition

Students can concentrate and focus on the execution of one specific task. These students are less capable of learning new material if they are required to multitask and consider multiple subjects and goals at once. They might also experience difficulty transitioning from one activity to another as their focus is extremely concentrated.

What do these definitions mean?

Students with a singular approach to learning prefer to concentrate and focus their attention on one task at a time.

Which behaviors may parents observe if their child demonstrates this learning issue?

- Your child becomes fixated on a specific task. They are not able to shift gears and move on to the next task.
- Transitions pose uncertainty and anxiety and they resist switching to a new activity.
- They focus well on one activity and experience difficulty incorporating new components into the activity in which they are already engaged.

Which professionals can treat this learning issue?

- Learning specialists
- Classroom teachers

Which teaching strategies can be effective in school?

- Allow students to divide their assignments into specific subject areas so only one skill base is being addressed.
- Model the steps of a learning task through completion for the students to refer back to as they move through their assignments.

Which strategies can help at home?

- Provide opportunities to incorporate new ways to expand upon a standard activity.

- Model different ways to complete assignments using varying strategies.

- Provide a written or pictorial schedule of the day so your child can prepare for anticipated transitions.

Concentrating on one component of a task at a time allows children to focus their attention while completing individual steps along the way.

 For additional resources or if you have a question, ask Dana at
EducationalAlternativesLLC.com/educational-advice

Visual Problem Solving

Clinical definition

Visual imagery plays an important role in the student's learning process. Students process primarily in images rather than in words.

Educators' definition

Difficulty solving problems or analyzing relationships when the information presented requires the person to imagine the scenario visually or spatially.

What do these definitions mean?

Creating mental images from stories, math problems, or science experiments is really hard for students with visual thinking difficulties. For example, if you ask these students to close their eyes and envision the word dog, they do not imagine a dog, but rather they see a blank page.

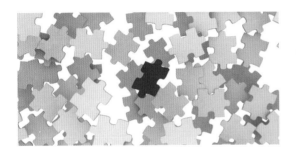

To some, piecing together a puzzle can be as difficult as understanding the visual images of letters, numbers, and words.

Which behaviors may parents observe if their child demonstrates this learning issue?

• Your child does not visually imagine shapes, stories, math problems, or other scenarios when they are described.

• Your child cannot describe what something looks like from imagination, and might describe the visual image as 'blank' when asked to do so.

• Children with visual/spatial learning problems frequently have trouble seeing the big picture, and often overlook the details as well.

Which professionals can treat this learning issue?

• Developmental optometrists
• Learning specialists
• Reading specialists

Visual graphic organizers enable students with visual problem solving issues to analyze relationships and to imagine topics visually and spatially that will foster solid connections.

Which teaching strategies can be effective in school?

- Use concrete examples to make connections with the real world.
- Incorporate experiential learning into lesson plans.
- Develop visual problem-solving skills and mental manipulation

> **Vocabulary**
>
> Experiential Learning: Learning through experience, or learning by reflecting on doing.

of information by having a hands-on component to your class presentations.

Which strategies can help at home?

- Incorporate hands on activities to bring mental images to life.
- Describe what you see and ask your child to help you describe the environment around you on a daily basis.
- Provide auditory description and details to formulate a picture of what is being discussed.
- Have your children make pictures, create story maps, and draw geometric shapes as a means of cultivating visual problem solving skills.

For additional resources or if you have a question, ask Dana at
EducationalAlternativesLLC.com/educational-advice

Working Memory

Clinical definition

Working memory, which is a basic executive function, refers to the instantaneous and temporary process of holding onto information, processing it, and manipulating it within a matter of seconds.

Educators' definition

Working memory refers to memory in the brain that is even shorter than short-term memory. These memories last a matter of seconds and they are important because they help people process incoming information, and form appropriate responses. When students struggle with working memory, they struggle to hold onto information temporarily, which makes processing and understanding all of the incoming information very difficult.

What do these definitions mean?

Since working memory is a necessary, and usually automatic, process that helps people understand and utilize new information, students with working memory issues have difficulty with a range of academic tasks and may also appear to have behavioral issues. It is possible to improve a person's working memory through targeted interventions.

Which behaviors may parents observe if their child demonstrates this learning issue?

• Your child struggles to follow spoken directions.

• It is difficult for your child to remember components of a multi-step problem.

• Recall of recently learned information is frequently inaccurate.

Which professionals can treat this learning issue?

• Learning specialists

• Classroom teachers

• Parents

Which teaching strategies can be effective in school?

• Reinforce what is being presented in class by incorporating multiple modalities.

• Provide graphs, charts, and maps to support students in following class lectures.

• Teach students to jot quick notes to remember key facts or instructions as they are presented.

• Offer students 'cheat sheets' with math facts, word banks, and visual graphic organizers.

Which strategies can help at home?

- Provide graphs, charts, and maps to support your child in completing homework assignments.

- Create separate fact sheets for math facts, word banks, and visual graphic organizers to jog their memory and formulate necessary connections.

- Review home fact sheets regularly.

- Teach your child to repeat back information as they receive it, or to say it aloud to themselves.

Sound working memory necessitates one's abiity to hold onto information long enough to process, incorporate, and form responses.

For additional resources or if you have a question, ask Dana at
EducationalAlternativesLLC.com/educational-advice

Written Language Skills

Clinical definition

Written language skills refer to a person's ability to use writing as a medium of effective communication. It entails the ability to encode letters into words and then into sentences generating a written message.

Educators' definition

A person who struggles with written language skills has difficulty relaying ideas in an organized and concise manner when asked to portray thoughts through writing. Vocabulary and ideas are presented in an overly simplistic manner. Summaries of content material are underdeveloped and lack direction.

What do these definitions mean?

Students with underdeveloped written language skills often use simple vocabulary, and their ideas may appear generalized and vague. Summaries of content material lack salient details and their work often lacks a clear thesis statement. Ideas presented may appear to lack logic or a cohesive sequence of events.

Which behaviors may parents observe if their child demonstrates this learning issue?

- Written vocabulary use is simplistic and underdeveloped.

- The ideas conveyed are basic and lack sophistication.

- The written format is without direction and lacks logical sequential order.

Which professionals can treat this learning issue?

- Learning specialists

- Classroom teachers

- Academic tutors

Which teaching strategies can be effective in school?

- Use graphic organizers that assist students with developing, arranging, and presenting assignments, ideas, and arguments.

- Provide a vocabulary list of common terms from content-based materials to help students incorporate these terms and ideas into their writing.

- Teach your students how to scaffold their own writing assignments so they don't have to start with a totally blank sheet of paper or computer screen.

Which strategies can help at home?

- Preplan all writing assignments.

- Create graphic organizers that contain the thesis statement, three topics for the body of the paper, and a concluding sentence. A structured outline fosters a logical sequence of events.

- Provide word banks for assigned topics enhancing the use and inclusion of age and subject appropriate vocabulary.

- Partner with your child and act as a scribe allowing for the flow of ideas to be easily transferred to paper.

- Incorporate the use of a Voice To Text (or Speech To Text) program. This allows children with written language difficulties to convey their thoughts verbally while speech recognition software simultaneously transcribes their words into a written format.

From hieroglyphics to modern writing, written language skills act as a medium of effective communication.

For additional resources or if you have a question, ask Dana at **EducationalAlternativesLLC.com/educational-advice**

TOPICS IN EDUCATION

Questions for Parent-Teacher Meetings

Is there a list of specific questions parents can use when preparing for parent-teacher meetings?

There is no specific list of questions to ask at a school because questions would vary widely with the profile of individual students. There are, however, questions that parents should ask that would help them to better understand how their children are performing in school.

Preparing questions to ask at a school meeting or at a parent-teacher conference would make the meetings more productive and lead to more informed outcomes.

Parents should also be prepared to offer insights as to their children's behavior, subject interests and dislikes, study patterns, time management and organizational skills, attention span on assignments, and how easily they tackle assignments from initiation to completion of tasks. Past experience in school and at home combined with professional feedback from school personnel could give parents a wealth of information that is beneficial to share at parent-teacher conferences.

Typically, teachers will begin the meeting by discussing your child's profile and progress. The goal of a parent-teacher conference is to understand your child's present level of performance. These meetings may be scheduled at the end of a marking period, or they may be scheduled to help decide how best to move forward in supporting your child at home and at school.

Finding out about your child's social abilities and about bullying, you may consider asking, "Is my son getting along well with his peers?"

If the answer is no, then ask the following:

- Is he sought out during structured or unstructured time?
- Does he have one or two friends with whom he feels comfortable?
- What steps are being taken to help him not be targeted by his peers?
- What can we do together to help foster his relationships with his peers?

Finding out about your child's social and academic abilities, you may consider asking, "Is my daughter participating in class discussions and activities?"

If the answer is no, then ask the following questions:

- Is she paying attention in class and is she engaged in lectures and assigned tasks?
- What are my child's strongest and weakest subjects?

- What are some examples of these strengths and weaknesses?

- How will my child be evaluated academically?

- What accommodations (such as the use of assistive technology—a calculator or electronic spell checker) can she use to complete assigned tasks?

- What can I do at home to help support her academic progress?

- What additional assistance or support do you recommend at this time to address the concerns that you have mentioned?

- At what point will the "Child Study Team" be brought together to discuss my child's profile and present level of performance?

The Child Study Team may consist of parents as well as the following professionals:
- **Classroom Teachers**
- **School Psychologists**
- **Principal**
- **Learning Specialists**
- **Speech and Language Pathologists**

- When should we meet again to discuss my concerns and to update my child's progress and performance?

As noted above, while there is no specific list of questions for parents to ask at school meetings, it is beneficial for parents to prepare a list of questions prior to formal meetings. It is recommended to take notes and to obtain a stated plan of action at the end of the meeting. It is most important that parents not leave any meeting unless they understand the next steps in securing the specific individualized needs of their child.

If you or school personnel believe that your child may require additional support and services in school, the next step would be to ask for an evaluation for a 504 Plan or an Individualized Education Program (commonly referred to by the letters IEP). Both 504 Plans and IEPs are explained on pages 82–86.

 For additional resources or if you have a question, ask Dana at
EducationalAlternativesLLC.com/educational-advice

Preparing for
Special Education Meetings

How can parents prepare for their child's special education meetings?

There are questions that parents should ask at CPSE (Committee for Preschool Special Education for children 3–5 years) or CSE (Committee on Special Education for students K–12) meetings that will help them to understand the process and implementation of a 504 Plan or Individualized Education Program (IEP) better.

Once you or the school believes that your child may require additional support and services in school, a meeting of the CPSE or CSE will convene to review your child's profile. There are several outcomes that can occur from this meeting, including a proposal to implement a 504 Plan or an IEP.

What is a 504 plan?

504 Plans provide building level support (support within the child's school) to assist children to bridge the gaps in their academic performance. This plan allows informal support for students with learning and attention issues who meet certain criteria.

The 504 Plan outlines how children's specific needs are met with accommodations, modifications, and other services. These measures are put into place in an attempt to remove barriers to learning.

With a 504 Plan, children stay within the general education setting throughout the day and participate in the general education curriculum. The general education teacher, the special education teacher, reading specialists, speech therapists, occupational therapists, and other professionals bring any necessary materials to the classroom and work directly with the student there.

Once your child is participating in a 504 Plan, there are steps you can take to help.

• If your child already has a 504 Plan, review his or her records. Understand the plan that is already in place. Review what you have and look for issues that need attention. Ask if your child is making progress or still struggling. Enquire about the support services that are (or are not) helpful.

• Think about any modifications and accommodations that may be helpful to students with 504 Plans. Are the modifications and accommodations that are in place for your child still useful? Do they need to be upgraded, replaced, or discontinued?

- Ask for clarification of any terms you hear during this meeting. You have the right to understand every detail of the decision.

- Make sure that the plan is complete and specific. Find out who is responsible for orchestrating this plan. Have their names included in the 504 Plan. Ask for a copy of the notes taken at the meeting.

- Request a copy of your child's new 504 Plan. Take this plan with you to your parent-teacher conferences.

After the 504 Plan meeting, how can parents follow up?

- Know who is providing your child's services. The 504 Plan should state not only what special services your child will receive but also the name of the person responsible for them. Ask your child periodically how working with Mr. Jones is going. Listen to the answers, and you will glean insight into how well the plan is being followed.

- Make sure that your child understands the services, including the assistive technology tools that he is entitled to use. Help him to self-advocate for the services outlined in the 504 Plan.

- Ask about the 504 Plan at parent-teacher conferences. Ask about your child's progress. Prepare questions prior to the meeting. Take notes. Have a plan of action. Do not leave your parent-teacher meeting until you understand the next steps. Ask for a copy of the notes from this meeting.

- Request a special team meeting if you are not satisfied with the results of your parent-teacher meeting and the implementation of the 504 Plan.

What is an IEP?

An IEP is a plan or program developed to ensure that a child who has a disability that is identified under the law receives specialized instruction and related services. Typically, children who require modifications to their curriculum will have an IEP, not a 504 Plan. Some children will be identified with a specific diagnosis ensuring that they receive an IEP. When preparing for an IEP meeting, you may want to do the following:

- Enquire as to the goal of this IEP meeting.
- Ask to have a copy of your child's most recent IEP document to follow along during the meeting.
- Ask for prior access to copies of the notes and reports that will be reviewed at the meeting.

During the IEP meeting, ask the following questions:

- How does everyone at the meeting know or work with my child?
- How is my child doing in making progress toward the IEP goals?
- What changes in goals would the team recommend?
- How will my child be assessed according to grade level?
- Who will work on that with my child? How? When? Where? How often?

- What does that accommodation and instructional intervention look like in the classroom?
- What can I do at home to support the IEP goals?
- I'd like to see the final IEP before agreeing to any changes suggested at this meeting. When can I see a copy?
- When will the changes to my child's program begin?
- Can we make a plan for keeping in touch about how everything is going?
- May I have a copy of the notes the teacher referenced during this meeting?
- If I have questions about the information I've been given about my child's rights, who is the person to talk to for answers?
- Who is the person to contact if I want to call another meeting?

As discussed above, there is no specific list of questions to ask at school meetings, but it is beneficial to prepare a list of questions prior to formal meetings, to take notes, and to obtain a stated plan of action. It is most important that parents not leave any meeting if they do not understand the next steps in securing the specific individualized needs of their child.

 For additional resources or if you have a question, ask Dana at **EducationalAlternativesLLC.com/educational-advice**

English Language Learners and Learning Disabilities

How can schools help English Language Learners who are also Learning Disabled?

Determining if English language learners (ELLs) are also learning disabled initially requires teacher observations and adaptations in class lessons. It also requires the administration of formal assessments in the students' native language and in English. Children who have difficulty in learning to read, write, and spell will have difficulty in both languages. Similar patterns of difficulty transcend languages. Understanding how to support ELLs who also have language-based learning disabilities is often difficult to determine because their struggle is often perceived as a language issue as opposed to a learning issue.

One of the factors that educators use in determining whether students have a learning disability is the low number of words students use. Educators observe that when teaching to their ELLs, students have developed their two languages either simultaneously or sequentially. Another factor is the amount of talking. Second language acquisition involves a non-verbal period where students are taking it all in. Sometimes this silence is viewed as a learning disability, but when tested in their native language, their supposed difficulty dissipates. It is often difficult to tease out whether ELLs have learning disabilities.

Bilingual speech pathologist Dr. Elsa Cardenas-Hagan emphasizes the importance of providing ELLs with an initial screening that can be used as an anchor in obtaining a baseline for proficiency in English. She recommends that educators incorporate strategies, make adjustments and adaptations in their instruction, monitor progress and if warranted, administer appropriate assessments by evaluators.

Once you know that a learning disability exists, an Individual Education Plan (IEP) needs to be developed that is specific to ELLs. The IEP needs to include what is the language of instruction, to state the guidelines for how the student is responding to specific goals and objectives, and to specify the adaptations that can be made in the classroom. It is also helpful to have students' native language incorporated into their lessons to support the goals and objectives stated in the IEPs, helping them to understand content-based information being presented in the classroom.

Effective teaching practices can help to facilitate fluency and literacy in academic and social language. These practices can include modeling through small group instruction, peer partners, books on tapes, and ELL support that complements the instruction being presented in the regular classroom. Peer assisted learning, differential instruction, and students being paired together all help to facilitate modeling where the language of the unit is emphasized in a relaxed manner. By presenting and practicing vocabulary, all students benefit. English language learners will respond positively to repetition and increase their understanding of the language and content being presented.

English language learners who are also learning disabled need to secure social language, academic language, and higher vocabulary skills in order to reach their academic goals. It is essential that the language of instruction in the classroom and the language of instruction for scaffolding support are consistent. Cultural differences play out in the classroom. Educators must be sensitive to the words they choose. A violin is a fiddle to some, and to others, the function of a dishwasher is unknown. Clarity of vocabulary requires social pragmatic language skills among peers and teachers. Incorporate opportunities for both each day.

It is essential that educators regularly monitor and assess comprehension of lessons being presented. In order for teachers to be both diagnostic and prescriptive, they need to analyze what is and what is not working when presenting their lessons. This is especially true with ELLs. Educators need to understand the challenges of their English language learners who are also learning disabled, implement their IEPs, and provide intensive instruction.

Educators will also benefit from welcoming the families of these ELLs into their schools and partnering with them in their quest to help their children learn to read, write, and spell. It would be helpful if home-school communication were written in the parents' native language, and that a person who spoke that native language were available to attend school meetings. Working effectively to help children with learning disabilities involves a home-school relationship. By promoting families to act as partners with their children's teachers, language fluency and literacy can be fostered, demonstrating yet another way that schools can help ELLs who are also learning disabled.

Watch TV in English with your children

Provide printed reading material

Set high academic expectations for your children

Home Strategies

Ensure steady school attendance

Communicate your concerns with your child's teachers

Foster cultural relationships and help break down language barriers with your school

For additional resources or if you have a question, ask Dana at
EducationalAlternativesLLC.com/educational-advice

Academic Anxiety with Regard to Performance and Transitions

How can schools help children deal with academic anxiety related to performance and transitions?

Many students struggle with academic anxiety. Educators often observe that performance anxiety can interfere with the learning process as these students tend to shut down and not 'hear' what is being presented. They also need sustained guidance for assignments and tests. Additionally, some students struggle with academic anxiety with regard to transitioning from one task to another. Educators often characterize such students as being ill-prepared for class and unable to begin the class period.

Effective teaching strategies and an open line of communication between the home and the school is essential to lowering the anxiety of these children. Parents need to be forthcoming with their understanding of their children's profiles, and educators need to be responsive to the angst that their students feel. Differential instruction will go a long way in helping students perform to their potential while reducing their anxiety.

With regard to performance anxiety, educators can create a structured setting where students are able to independently

negotiate their academic work by
seeking out assistance and utilizing
specific learning strategies. They
can lower the level of uncertainty
of their students by providing

an academic framework and by offering direct instruction to
students before beginning independent writing assignments.
Educators who provide detailed outlines from which to study
and consult when completing assignments and preparing for
tests give these students a visual framework from which to refer.

For students who display academic anxiety with regard to
transitions, educators can state clear expectations of the class
lesson and the assigned work, making sure that directions are
both verbally and visually presented. If students understand
what is expected, it greatly assists them in dealing
with anxiety-producing situations. For younger
children, class charts on the wall stating rules
of behaviors and academic expectations provide
parameters and a framework.

Empower your children by reminding them to be proactive
and self-promoters in their classroom and to develop and
hone specific strategies that they can incorporate into their

assignments. This is an excellent way to build students' self-confidence and increase their sense of control over their anxiety. Parents also need to remain

supportive while their children complete assigned tasks at home as stress is frequently associated with academic anxiety.

There are numerous ways in which students can negotiate and navigate their school day with decreased anxiety. Parental understanding of their children's profiles, effective teaching strategies and a concentrated effort on the part of these students can blend together in a positive and effective manner, allowing the school to help students lessen academic anxiety with regard to performance and to transitions.

For additional resources or if you have a question, ask Dana at
EducationalAlternativesLLC.com/educational-advice

Tips for Children with Poor Executive Function Skills

What Tips Can You Offer Children with Poor Executive Function Skills?

Students who exhibit executive functioning challenges need to prioritize the most important steps required to complete assignments. They need to plan ahead, thinking about the steps necessary to organize their time, and estimating how much time each step may take to complete.

According to researchers at the Harvard's Center on the Developing Child, executive function allows us to manage ourselves and access our resources in order to achieve a specific task. It involves both mental control and self-regulation. The Center describes executive function and self-regulation skills as the mental processes that enable us to plan, focus attention, remember instructions, and juggle multiple tasks successfully. In their literature, they describe three types of brain function: working memory, mental flexibility, and self-control:

• Working memory allows us to retain and manipulate distinct pieces of information over short periods of time.

- Mental flexibility helps us to sustain shifting our attention in response to different demands or to apply different rules in different settings.
- Self-control enables us to set priorities and resist impulsive actions or response.

Students with executive function challenges will benefit from organizing their materials before they start work on a project. With long-term assignments, students should initiate a plan in a timely fashion. During the interval between initiation and completion of a task, students need to complete multiple steps and use great diligence, which is often daunting and overwhelming. To succeed, students must be persistent and mindful of each section of a specific task with the strength to forge ahead as they complete interim steps along the way.

When students feel frustrated and experience performance anxiety, they may find it helpful to keep their cool by regulating their emotions and trying a 'smash the task' approach. Using this technique, students can break down assignments into manageable components. In this way, they lessen their angsts while demonstrating progress in completing assigned tasks.

Students also benefit from the ability to think flexibly in their approach to an assignment so they can change their strategies when needed. Controlling impulsive reactions allows them to think before they act and to keep distractions in check. By stopping, thinking and then acting, students are able to assess their options, which allows them to make sound decisions. Students need to learn how to transition from one task to another when they have completed one portion of an assigned task and need to initiate work on other parts.

Understanding how to navigate and negotiate assignments permits students to work efficiently and effectively from initiation to completion of tasks. By using some of the strategies described above, children will improve their executive function skills. Ultimately, this will enhance the likelihood that your children will complete assignments to the best of their ability.

Source: Executive Function & Self-Regulation. Center on the Developing Child at Harvard University

For additional resources or if you have a question, ask Dana at
EducationalAlternativesLLC.com/educational-advice

Motor Skills, Visual Perception Skills, and Academic Readiness

What is the relationship between motor and visual perceptual skills? And how do difficulties in these areas impede academic readiness in school?

While motor and visual perceptual skills are often closely associated, they can be separate and distinct. An individual with a motor problem does not necessarily have a visual perceptual problem. Trying to discern the difference is the reason that specific assessments are administered. Tests using a motor requirement are assessing visual-motor integration, and are therefore sometimes thought to measure visual perception. The Motor-Free Visual Perception Test, developed by Colarusso and Hammill, assesses spatial relationship, visual discrimination, figure ground, visual closure, and visual use of a motor component.

Specific information is obtained through each of the above subtests. **Spatial relationship** assesses the ability to orient one's body in space and to perceive the positions of objects in relation to oneself and to other objects. An example of this includes the reversal of letters or patterns in relation

Spatial Relationship

to one another. **Visual discrimination** assesses the ability to discriminate dominant features in different objects. Examples of this include the ability to discriminate position, forms, and letter-like forms. **Figure ground** assesses the ability to distinguish an object from its background. **Visual closure** assesses the ability to identify incomplete figures when only fragments are presented. Examples of this include being able to identify partially completed familiar objects such as dogs, cats, and various shapes. **Visual memory** assesses the ability to recall dominant features of one stimulus. This is closely related to visual short-term memory. Short-term memory is assessed by requiring the child to reproduce a geometric figure from memory. Visual sequential memory is assessed by requiring the child to place in order a sequence of non-symbolic figures from memory.

Visual Discrimination

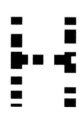

Figure Ground

Visual Closure

Activities such as matching pictures help children develop visual memory.

Children's abilities to correctly copy geometric forms correlate significantly with their academic development. Correlations have been noted between form-copying tests and readiness tests in Kindergarten and between copying and early reading achievement. Children can have well developed visual and motor skills but be unable to integrate the two. The VMI (Developmental Test of Visual Motor Integration), which was developed by Beery and Buktenica, has demonstrated academic correlations in reading and math in primary-age children.

The relationship between perceptual development and conceptual development is crucial to understanding the relationship between motor and visual perceptual skills and how it affects learning. Some specialists theorize that adequate conceptual development is dependent upon appropriate perceptual development. Perceptual motor match involves the coordination of the eyes and hands. In fact, Kephardt, a leading developmentalist in this field, believes that motor development precedes visual development.

If your children are having difficulty with pen-and-paper tasks, in visually identifying or recognizing objects, or in remembering specific patterns or sequences, it is appropriate to explore whether they are exhibiting visual or motor perceptual difficulties. Raise your concerns with their teachers and ask that the Motor-Free Visual Perception Test and the VMI be administered to ascertain specific information that will be needed in helping to identify any potential difficulty that can be remediated through direct intervention.

An activity to hone visual discrimination skills could be to have children identify the similarities and differences between the above two illustrations.

For additional resources or if you have a question, ask Dana at
EducationalAlternativesLLC.com/educational-advice

Using Modalities When Learning New Concepts and Tasks

What are learning modalities and how do they help children to integrate and assimilate information when learning a new concept or task?

Learning modalities are the visual, auditory, or kinesthetic ways in which we learn. Each of us has a preferred way of learning a concept or a task. We are, in essence, visual, auditory, or kinesthetic learners. Some people learn best by watching, some by listening, and others by actively participating in specific tasks being presented. The concept of learning modalities remains the same whether a person is learning how to make a batch of brownies, ski down steep slopes, or change a tire. We each have a preference to watch, listen, or actively participate in what we are being taught.

Typically, people favor one modality over another. However, students who are both visual and auditory learners have an easier time in school, as classes tend to be lecture-based with visual components that augment specific lessons. Educators are aware that children favor one modality over another and often incorporate a multi-modality approach to their lessons through differential instruction.

The VAKT approach to teaching (visual, auditory, kinesthetic and tactile) allows educators to tap into their students' preferred learning modality while simultaneously helping them to integrate and assimilate new concepts and tasks. A VAKT approach to teaching, for example, includes students being presented with a vocabulary word (visual), while hearing their teacher say the vocabulary word (auditory). Students then "sky write" the word that has been written for them and feel the movement of their hands in conjunction with the touch of pen to paper (kinesthetic and tactile).

The rationale behind the VAKT method in the above example is that by including as many senses as possible, students are being given additional sensory experiences or cues to help them learn the vocabulary word being presented. If students are weak in one or two modalities, the other modalities help to convey the necessary information.

In young children, tactile stimulation associated with visual stimuli can enhance reading readiness. Some reading clinicians see reading as a visual-motor skill, and not only as a visual discrimination skill. For example, children respond faster to learning their letter sounds when they work with sandpaper letters, rather than smooth painted letters.

VAKT skills also assist in learning basic computational skills as well as counting. Educational theorists have discovered that providing objects to manipulate and demonstrate problem solutions improved children's computational performance. Finger counting, for instance, is part of many arithmetic programs.

Touching and moving objects without appropriate verbal accompaniment are not sufficient. Nor is verbally saying the numbers in order without understanding the corresponding verbal-motor performance. However, once a coordinated verbal-motor repertoire is learned, then it is appropriate for the verbal component alone to be extended meaningfully. For example, after children have learned to count ten objects, just a verbal response in counting to 20 will be sufficient.

If your children demonstrate a particular strength or weakness with regard to their learning modalities, it is appropriate to inform their teachers because it is easier to learn a new concept or task when presented from a modality of strength. If you want to know more about your child's learning modality, have the Swassing-Barbe Modality Index administered to identify the child's modality preference. When you understand how your child learns best, he or she can then be given this information to self-advocate to the point of saying to a teacher, "Please show me, tell me, let me try it," when presented with a new concept or task.

 For additional resources or if you have a question, ask Dana at
EducationalAlternativesLLC.com/educational-advice

Adapting Homes for Learning Disabled Children

How can parents adapt their homes to support their learning disabled children?

Children who have been classified as learning disabled and who attend public school receive special education services in school. Assuming that learning disabled children receive help for their cognitive and perceptual difficulties during school hours, the question that arises is: "What happens to these children after 3:00 pm?" The difficulties that they encounter go home with them! Therefore, if these children have right-left directionality problems, then they could have difficulty using the stovetop or deciphering hot and cold on faucets. If they reverse their numbers in school, then they could reverse them dialing, or in setting an alarm clock. This article discusses how parents can support their children within their own home.

Children who have problems associated with learning disabilities may be able to function more efficiently and successfully in the various rooms of their home if there have been physical adaptations of their home environment. After all, up to half their time is spent within the home. Organization is essential for the optimal physical environment of the home. Since most of these youngsters lack organizational skills, structure must come from elsewhere. To facilitate their children's development, parents must act as teachers at home and rethink the use of appliances, for example, and the physical space of their homes.

Physical adaptations do not necessarily improve visual-perceptual, spatial-relation, auditory-perceptual, or tactile-kinesthetic skills. These physical adaptations, however, allow many children to use each room of their home efficiently and successfully.

The populations that will most likely benefit from the physical adaptation of their home are children who have trouble with right-left directionality, spatial-relationship, and organizational skills.

As a child, I experienced some of the above challenges and had a great deal of difficulty using appliances correctly. I provide the following suggestions to help children who experience similar difficulties.

Children who have right-left directionality problems and attempt to operate both electric and gas ranges often become greatly confused. The numerous gadgets surrounding the perimeters of the ranges are bewildering to some learning disabled children. Some stoves list the burners as LF, LR, RF, and RR. These letters stand for Left Front, Left Rear, Right Front, and Right Rear. For children who have right-left directionality problems, this labeling is worthless. Simple adaptations made by parents and placed on the ranges would eliminate confusion and foster their child's independence. Parents can color code their stoves for easy-to-use directions. Make the right side red and the left side blue. In black write the letters F and B for front and back. Place these cards on the wall directly above the stove. Children with right-left directionality problems will gradually learn to associate their right side with red and their left side with blue. Children with spatial-relationship challenges will use the color-coded charts to orient themselves.

How kitchen and bathroom cabinets, closets, and drawers are organized is essential for learning disabled children. The proper arrangement will enable them to easily locate specific articles. Children with poor spatial-relationship challenges, short-term memory issues, and figure-ground problems all need organization of space in order to locate particular items. To organize drawers, use compartmentalized or divided drawers.

The dividers for storing flatware in the kitchen are perfect for organizing drawers in the bathroom. This system of organizing your kitchen and bathroom cabinets, closets, and drawers will greatly aid in your children's ability to find what they are seeking.

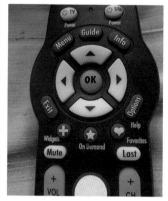

Children who have problems associated with learning disabilities may be able to function more efficiently and successfully in the various rooms of their residence if there have been physical adaptations of their home environment.

For additional resources or if you have a question, ask Dana at
EducationalAlternativesLLC.com/educational-advice

School Suspensions

Is it true that school suspensions are on the rise?

Yes, school suspensions are absolutely on the rise. New standards of behavior and expectations of students from kindergarten through 12th grade are in place in both private and public schools. The number of children who are suspended for nonviolent acts is alarming. In one case, a kindergartner was suspended for calling his teacher "a dumb bunny!" Because suspensions have adverse effects on our children, we need to develop solutions, not suspensions.

Lisa Syron, the executive director of Student Advocacy, and Stefanie Shabman, the legal director of the same organization provided statistics in "Solutions Not Suspensions," a presentation that Student Advocacy gave on the topic. The group's findings reveal that more than 100,000 students were suspended from New York City's schools in the 2011–2012 school year, representing four percent of the student population. An estimated 78 percent of the suspensions in grades 11–12 in New York City and 94 percent of the suspensions in Westchester County, New York were for nonviolent incidents.

Alarmingly, 22 percent of all suspended children are elementary school students. Statistics indicate that disabled students are far more likely to be suspended than their nondisabled counterparts.

School suspensions lead to loss of academic time and, often, to academic failure. Syron and Shabman report that among students suspended from New York City during the 2011–2012 school year, 31 percent were held back compared with five percent of students who were not suspended.

Sadly, school suspensions nationally are a gateway into the juvenile justice system. A three-day suspension plus 20 additional absences has been correlated to a 61 percent increase in arrest rates among students. Schools in this scenario are a prison pipeline.

Clearly, faculty training is needed to foster acceptance of best practices in working with disabled students. Administrations need to review each case prior to a school suspension to determine if an alternative solution can be put into place. For instance, an elementary school student who has an auditory processing disorder may not 'hear' the command to 'remove his hat' in the hallway by his teacher or principal. The hallway may offer too many external distractions for the student to 'tune' into that instruction. So, even though hats are not allowed to be worn in school, and despite the fact that this child may have been asked repeatedly to 'remove his hat,' a suspension for insubordination would be an unreasonable solution for that student.

Alternative solutions to suspensions are crucial because students often make poor decisions and their social judgment is not sound. After all, students are children, and educational institutions need to embrace these situations as teachable moments, not punitive ones. Examples that Syron and Shabman suggest as alternative solutions to suspensions included community service and a campaign to show the harm of smoking when caught smoking on school grounds. With regard to alcohol use, they suggest weekly in-school detentions with group counseling in alcoholism and addiction.

Another suggestion for alternative responses for disciplinary offenses is restoration justice–making amends for inappropriate action and having the punishment fit the crime. Other suggestions include reflective essays making apologies and taking ownership for the actions, as well as parent meetings, community service, and withdrawal of privileges. Examples of preventative measures that will also help to avoid suspensions include training by mental health professionals who will instruct faculty on how to deescalate situations. Mediation, academic support, credit recovery, mentoring coaches, and actively teaching social skills and character development will all aid in reducing the increase in school suspensions.

Let school suspensions become teachable moments. Alternative solutions to suspensions can include community service when caught on school grounds defacing the buildings with graffiti.

 For additional resources or if you have a question, ask Dana at **EducationalAlternativesLLC.com/educational-advice**

Accommodations and Interventions in Private Schools

Are independent schools required to provide accommodations and interventions specified in formal psychoeducational evaluations such as extended time or do they have a choice in what services they choose to provide?

Private schools, unlike public institutions, do not need to follow the same guidelines and implementation of educational services as do their public counterparts because they are not legally required to do so. Independent schools are not under any obligation to implement 504 Plans or Independent Education Plans (IEPs). The explanations of classified diagnoses and the subsequent accommodations and interventions stated in these reports are written for public schools only and for public access to educational institutions, but not for independent schools. Independent schools, however, are under an obligation to consider the stated recommendations presented in formal evaluations of their students. Whether your child is enrolled in public or private schools, parents need to understand the importance of establishing and maintaining a paper trail based on findings in formal evaluations in order to obtain for their child any accommodations and interventions.

All private schools that do not service children with identified special needs have a choice in determining which accommodations, if any, they are comfortable providing. Parents, for the most part, understand this when they enroll their children. School policies and procedures are listed on school websites. The reason that private schools are not required to implement accommodations recommended in formal evaluations is that the American Disability Act (ADA) does not apply to independent schools. In fact, with regard to independent schools, the ADA's position is that private schools are under an obligation to consider recommendations, but not to grant them.

The culture of each individual private school dictates the policies that these schools will follow rather than Federal and State guidelines dictating the implementation of services to children who meet eligibility. The most common accommodation provided to students in independent schools is extended time. Some schools offer untimed testing to all students, but some students need to jump through hoops in order to be afforded extended time on tests. A recent review of several independent day schools in New York City revealed that 15–35% of Upper School students receive extended time.

The crucial decision point for parents of children who have not received services to date, but now want to assert their voice in this area, is when it is time to petition the College Board and ACT for extended time. It has become apparent at numerous private day schools that many parents whose children's academic performance is solid seek documentation that supports a request to the College Board or ACT for extended time. They often seek these accommodations by having evaluations administered privately to their children and then applying directly to the College Board or ACT, bypassing their schools.

Some independent schools counsel parents to be careful in asking for accommodations because their children may not get into the college of their choice if perceived as learning disabled. Medical diagnoses of an Anxiety Disorder and/or an Adjustment Disorder are sometimes presented by parents as reasons for extended time when educational reasons are not sufficient. In these instances, the role and the responsibilities of independent schools vary. Some independent schools support these diagnoses and help to appeal decisions being made by the College Board and ACT. Other independent schools will facilitate an appeal, but often without additional evidence to support the case being presented.

In some instances, it is not helpful for students to receive extended time and sit 4 ½–6 hours to take a test that is typically administered in 3 hours. Parents need to understand the consequences of their requests and to understand the differences between the SAT and ACT with regard to testing accommodations. For example, ACT will divide up their tests by sections; SAT will not. The College Board does not give testing over multiple days; ACT will. But, most importantly, parents and independent schools need to understand that the accommodation of extended time on standardized tests is in place to level the playing field for all students, not just to give certain individuals a greater chance for success.

If your children are enrolled in independent schools, become familiar with their policies and procedures regarding how the schools incorporate accommodations and interventions based upon formal evaluations. Participate in ongoing dialogues with the administration and faculty to ensure that the school meets your child's individual needs while remaining true to the culture of the school. Clearly, a paper trail attesting to a specific area of concern is essential in obtaining extended time in school and on standardized tests such as the SAT and ACT.

For additional resources or if you have a question, ask Dana at
EducationalAlternativesLLC.com/educational-advice

How to Transition Smoothly to College with Learning Issues

How can students with learning differences successfully prepare and transition to college?

Many students with learning differences have Individual Education Programs that identify specific diagnosis and state appropriate accommodations affording each individuals to reach their academic potential. Along the way, these students have had cheerleaders as professionals cheering them on and motivating them to succeed to the best of their ability. They have had assistance in time management, organization and planning, initiation of assigned tasks, and checkpoints ensuring completion of these tasks. They have also been provided with word banks, study guides, readers when necessary, books on tapes, calculators, scribes, and numerous tools that have fostered their skillset and academic performance.

However, once it is time for college, these very students who have successfully negotiated and navigated their way through high school now need to prepare for how they are going to self-advocate for their individual needs in an environment without an Individual Education Program. Transitioning from high school to college with learning differences can be seamless if preparation and protocol are followed.

The key to a successful transition is communication and transparency. Once accepted and committed to a college, students need to obtain a current psychoeducational or neuropsychological evaluation. Evaluations older than three years are not considered current. Then they need to notify Student Disabilities Services on Campus. This conversation is best to take place prior to the beginning of the fall semester. Planning and implementation of specific accommodations as well as the selection of appropriate courses is essential. By partnering with Disability Services, qualified students will receive equal access to their education, appropriate accommodations, and assistance in ways to self-advocate.

At most colleges and universities, students will be asked to complete an ADA Intake Form. ADA stands for the American Disability Act and by filling out this form, students begin the process to receive individual accommodations based upon recommendations made in their formal evaluations. The Intake Form asks what accommodations are being requested. Common requests include extended time, preferential seating, taking tests in a quiet and separate location, books on tape, and use of a calculator.

There is another section on The Intake Form that asks students to describe how their disability "Currently impacts and substantially limits your academic work, class schedule, class location and/or residential living situation." It also asks to "Include previous accommodations received plus accommodations that you think you will need on a college level."

Colleges often provide an orientation prior to the start of school as a means for students to settle in and meet people prior to the arrival of the full student body and the commencement of classes. It is during this time that new students and their parents can make appointments with the office of Student Disability Services, and receive guidance from a counselor who has had the opportunity to read and review individual formal evaluations and Intake Forms. During the course of this conversation, specific requests for accommodations can be made. A discussion will then ensue with other members on the Committee of students with disabilities, and in a short amount of time, students will receive written notification explicitly stating what accommodations have been approved.

It is important that students maintain copies of their accommodation letter. "At the beginning of each term, a student must request their accommodation letters for faculty, staff, and campus officials. The student will deliver the accommodation letters in a timely manner prior to the need of the accommodation. Accommodations are not retroactive, so students are encouraged to request accommodation letters the first week of classes. Accommodations are in place only after the student notifies the instructor and discusses arrangements to be made."

The key to a successful transition is communication and transparency. By partnering with Disability Services on campus, qualified students will receive equal access to their education, appropriate accommodations, and assistance in ways to self-advocate.

In addition to specific accommodations being given to qualified students, college professors, writing centers, and learning excellence programs are available on campuses allowing additional support for each and every student who seeks guidance.

Source: High Point University, Office of Accessibility Resources and Services: highpoint.edu/disabilitysupport/

 For additional resources or if you have a question, ask Dana at **EducationalAlternativesLLC.com/educational-advice**

Social-Emotional Challenges LD Students Face in the College Application Process

How can we as parents help our learning disabled (LD) student deal with the social-emotional side of applying to colleges?

The social-emotional component of learning disabled (LD) students when applying to colleges is often fraught with fear and apprehension beyond what their non-LD peers experience. After all, the application process demands solid skills in executive functioning, organization, time management, processing speed, reading comprehension skills, written language skills, working memory, and mature social judgment.

LD candidates often worry that they are unable to meet expectations and feel overwhelmed when moving through the various stages of the college application process. There are, however, useful tips and advice. Breaking the large process down into manageable steps will make possible a successful entry into college. Below are ten helpful ways in which parents can assist their LD children in the college application process.

1. Many parents are familiar with only the "cocktail circuit schools" and do not understand that these schools may not be

appropriate choices for their children. They need to distinguish between what makes a good college and what makes a college a good match for the LD candidate. Parents must be reminded that because a school is unfamiliar, it doesn't mean it is not a good choice for their child.

2. The SATs are process-oriented tests. The ACTs are product-oriented tests. If your child understands a specific subject matter, then the ACT is the one to choose. However, both the SATs and the ACTs are standardized tests and pose difficulty for LD students. As parents, it is important to tell your child that SATs and ACTs should not and cannot define one's self worth. These standardized tests do not demonstrate students' academic potential.

> **Vocabulary**
>
> Process-Oriented Test: A test where students extrapolate information to answer a question.
>
> Product-Oriented Test: A test that focuses on specific content-based knowledge.

3. Teach your LD child that his or her SAT and ACT performances are not accurate predictors of success. Rather success in life can often be measured by the following characteristics:

- Resilience

- Optimism and enthusiasm

- Dedication

- Motivation

- Time management skills

- Perseverance

- Connection to community, friends, and family

- Appreciation of life and the ability to enjoy the moment.

4. Tell your child to be honest about whom he or she is. The right college match cannot be found if there is a shroud of pretention. Parents must stress the importance of helping their children maintain their voice throughout the application process. Teach your children never to speak ill of themselves. Everyone has strengths and vulnerabilities, and students do not need to draw attention to their vulnerabilities.

5. Extracurricular activities may be limited for LD candidates compared with their peers due to the need for academic tutoring after school in more than one subject as well as for more time to complete homework assignments. This may be an opportunity to emphasize character strengths that allow your LD child to distinguish themselves as strong student body members citing their determination to persevere and diligence as key qualities to possess as individuals.

6. LD students frequently have a difficult time self-advocating. Encourage your children to feel pro-active and self-sufficient. Helping them to develop interview strategies is an excellent way to foster resilience in students, to build confidence, and for them to feel in control of the application process.

7. Create a list of questions that will help your children select appropriate colleges. Questions should be self-reflective and may include:

- How do I learn best?
- What level of support do I require?
- What assistive technology will be beneficial in meeting my individual needs?

8. Identify the culture of the college community that is the best match for your child? Ask:

- Do I want a traditional or non-traditional environment?
- Which activities, clubs, and sports are offered?
- What is weekend life like?
- Are there religious affiliations?
- What about athletic opportunities?
- What academic support is available?
- What counseling options are there?
- What types of assistive technology are accepted?
- Are there community service opportunities?

9. The college essay is often a source of contention between parents and their LD children. As parents, read your child's college essay for spelling and grammar errors alone. Let the authentic voice of the applicant emerge. Use phrases such as, "Did you consider mentioning A, B, or C? I think that a college may want to know that about you," as Merilee Jones states in her book *Less Stress, More Success*. She advises to "simply point out the positive; don't attempt to package the candidate into a product you hope the college will buy."

10. Have your LD students take psychoeducational and neuropsychological tests in their senior year after the college application process is completed. This will allow them to have accommodations and interventions for the first three years of college and they will not have to juggle these tests while taking the SATs and or ACTs.

Understanding the individual needs of your LD child is essential in determining the appropriate college and forging solid matches for LD students. Your children's social-emotional wellbeing is contingent upon this research as well as the opportunity for academic and personal success.

Adapted from "Insights," The Newsletter of the Independent Educational Consultants Association, April/May 2016.

For additional resources or if you have a question, ask Dana at
EducationalAlternativesLLC.com/educational-advice

When Children Are at a Career or Vocational Crossroad

How can parents help to guide their children when they are at a career or vocational crossroad?

Do your children know what they want to major at college? Do they presently possess a skill set that would enable them to seek and secure employment? Are they in their twenties and still dabbling in a variety of jobs? Do they appear directionless? If so, they may benefit from participating in an online career guidance tool that will help them learn about themselves and identify their long-term career interests.

By highlighting an individual's natural abilities, interests, personalities, and values/lifestyles, this online tool will make appropriate career choices apparent. A career guidance tool can help to foster smart education decisions, identify the right internships, build a resume of relevant accomplishments, and find a job right out of high school or college.

Crossroads are always challenging. Transitioning from one phase to another poses a certain level of uncertainty. Being able to identify college and career paths greatly reduces the level of uncertainty and helps to define how best to obtain the education or specific skill set needed to secure future employment.

Scores of young people can be helped to define their career paths through an online assessment tool administered by a licensed practitioner. One such tool is The Greenwood System 120™. The GS120 is a career and guidance tool that measures a person's abilities, interests, values, and personality. It matches that profile to a database of over 1000 jobs to find the best 10 percent matches. This system depends upon a trained counselor or advisor to help an individual go through a self-exploration and career exploration process to narrow the list to the very best career matches for each individual.

There are numerous personality/career tools that are not well grounded in their research. The GS120, however, combines the Myers-Briggs, the Holland Codes, and a Grit Score to help assess values and motivators as well as personality characteristics and provides a defined list of well-matched careers and academic paths.

The Myers-Briggs Type Indicator is an introspective self-report questionnaire designed to indicate psychological preferences in how people perceive the world and make decisions. The Holland Codes refers to a theory of careers and vocational choice based on personality types. Grit is defined as perseverance and passion for long-term goals.

Individuals who participate in The Greenwood System online assessment can glean a great deal about where their interests lie and what they need to do to secure a career in an identified area of interest.

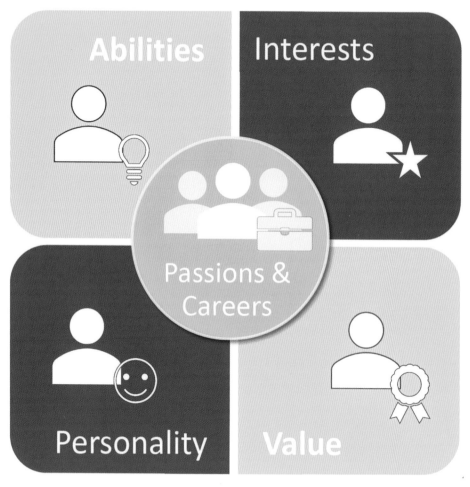

The Greenwood System 120 analyzes data to identify passions and optimum career paths.

 For additional resources or if you have a question, ask Dana at **EducationalAlternativesLLC.com/educational-advice**

RESOURCES

Sample Parent Letter to Request School Evaluation

Request for evaluation

If you observe that your child is experiencing learning issues and would like the school to administer formal testing, you can write a letter to the school principal similar to the one below. Replace what is in red with your own text.

Sample letter

Marta Smith
3333 Lakeside Drive
Katonah, NY 10536

Jose Marti Elementary School
578 North Main Street
Katonah, NY 10536

October 15, 2018

Dear Principal Jones,

I am writing to you today regarding my increased concern for my son, _____.
He is experiencing challenges within the classroom and at home that to date are adversely affecting his academic performance. I am requesting that a complete psychoeducational evaluation be administered. It is my sincere hope that the findings provide us with educational strategies to help him feel more comfortable and confident in his classes.

Please let me know what I can do to help facilitate this process. I am available to discuss my concerns further at a team meeting where his teachers can share their observations and we can begin to understand the reasons he is struggling in school.

Sincerely,

Marta Smith

cc: name of classroom teacher
    name of the director of support services

Tips for composing the letter

When composing the letter, please note the following points:

- Sometimes parents' concerns are academic, behavioral, or attention related. State your concerns and describe your observations. Speak in the first person and remember that a successful path requires a partnership with your school. Remain positive and request what you want. After all, parents are their children's advocates.

- Once the school receives a written letter requesting that a psychoeducational evaluation be administered, the school has 30 days in which to start to carry out this request.

In search of a diagnosis and treatment plan

- Before a student can receive special education services, he or she must be evaluated for eligibility. Under the Individuals with Disabilities Education Act (IDEA), the categories under which a child can receive these services include the following:

    1. Autism spectrum disorder

    2. Deafness

    3. Deaf-blindness

    4. Emotional disturbance (examples include anxiety disorders, schizophrenia, obsessive/compulsive disorder)

5. Hearing impairment (the type of hearing loss that can vascilate over time)

6. Intellectual disability (a cognitive disability for children who have reduced cognitive abilities such as children with down syndrome)

7. Multiple disabilities (a child who meets eligibility for more than one condition under the IDEA)

8. Orthopedic impairment caused by congenital anomaly, by disease (bone tuberculosis, for example), and from other causes (cerebral palsy and amputation, for example)

9. Other health impairment (examples include ADHD and asthma and other conditions that adversely affect learning)

10. Specific learning disability (examples include dyslexia, dyscalculia, dysgraphia, auditory processing disorder, nonverbal learning disabilities)

11. Speech or language impairment (communication problems such as stuttering, impaired articulation)

12. Traumatic brain injury

13. Visual impairment

(Source: Center for Parent Information and Resources.
Categories of Disability Under IDEA. Newark, N.J.)

- If the Committee of Special Education determines that your child meets the criteria to be classified, discussion will center upon the appropriate services your child is entitled to receive. If your child is to receive special services, it is advisable to ask pertinent questions such as the following:
  — What will his daily schedule look like?
  — What push-in or pull-out services will he receive?
  — What is the frequency and duration of these services?
  — How will his progress be measured and determined?
- If the school has stated that attention, anxiety, or auditory processing issues appear to be an area of concern, it is important to understand that a school cannot diagnosis ADHD, a Generalized Anxiety Disorder, or an Auditory Processing Disorder. These are medical diagnoses and need to be determined through a neurologist, a child psychiatrist, or a speech and language pathologist.
- Schools can address the learning issues of medical diagnoses, but it is optimal for medical and school personnel to work in unison to develop treatment plans for students who meet the criteria of a formal diagnosis.
- Not every student with learning or attention issues qualifies with a disability under IDEA.

Glossary

Academic Readiness: The state of a student's preparedness to learn new concepts.

Accommodations: A term used in an Individualized Education Program (IEP) or a 504 Plan that describes a change in how a student performs a certain learning task. For example, if students have reduced processing speed, an accommodation may allow them to have extra time on standardized tests.

Active Learning: An approach to learning in which students engage and participate in the learning process.

ADA Intake Form/Questionnaire: Forms a student obtains from a college or university's office of academic support services in order to receive accommodations while studying at a higher-level institution. The ADA (American Disabilities Act) allows students to request specific disability support services. Students are responsible to provide professional documentation of their disability.

Addition Facts: Addition problems whose addends are whole numbers—

Addends	Sum
$2 + 8 =$	10
$109 + 2 =$	111

not fractions, not decimals—from 0 through 10 as well as extensions with 10, 100, etc. Examples: $2 + 2 = 4$, $10 + 10 = 20$, $5 + 3 = 8$, $105 + 8 = 113$, $0 + 1000 = 1000$

Assistive Technology: Any device—such as a calculator, recording device, or audiobook—that helps students complete their schoolwork to the best of their ability.

Associative Learning: An approach to learning in which ideas and experiences reinforce each other and can be linked to one another.

Auditory: Pertaining to the sense of hearing.

Auditory Information: Information obtained by hearing, which is then processed in the brain and used to make relevant interpretations. See *listening comprehension.*

Auditory Working Memory: A mental process that keeps the information that people hear for a short period of time.

Basic Number Facts: Addition problems whose addends are whole numbers from 0 through 10; subtraction problems whose minuends are whole numbers from 0 through 20 and whose subtrahends are whole numbers from 0 through 10; multiplication problems whose factors are whole numbers from o through 10; and division problems whose dividends are whole numbers between 0 through 100, whose divisors are whole numbers between 0 and 10, and whose quotients are whole numbers. See *addition facts, subtraction facts, multiplication facts,* and *division facts.*

Brainstorming: A technique used to begin writing an essay or plan a long-term project where you come up with as many new ideas as possible in order to select the strongest concepts and notice important connections between and among ideas.

Call-and-Response Technique: A teaching technique that is similar to a question and answer format that is performed rapidly. In a structured manner, the leader calls out while the group listens to the call, processes the message, and responds in unison. Many times this technique is used to transition between subjects and to demonstrate preparedness.
Examples: The leader claps a beat. The group responds by clapping a similar beat. The teacher sings "Students, students, are you ready?" The students reply by singing, "Teacher, teacher, we are ready!"

Chunking Information: Chunking refers to pulling specific material from context in order to facilitate understanding.

Information in this context refers to remembering content in manageable chunks, thus chunking information refers to improving a person's ability to process and remember information.

Computational Accuracy: Ability to calculate a mathematical equation and arrive at the correct answer.

Constructive Criticism: Offering or receiving valid and well-reasoned opinions about performance and behavior. The comments can be positive or negative and they are meant to improve the person's performance or behavior in the future.

Critical Thinking: A form of learning, thought, and analysis that goes beyond memorizing and recalling facts. It is a form of learning that includes analysis, evaluation, interpretation, and synthesis of information and the application of creative thought to solve a problem or reach a conclusion.

Decoding: The practice of using various reading skills to translate written words on a page into sounds when read aloud. When decoding, people sound out unknown words by pronouncing their parts and then joining the parts together to form cohesive words.

Differential Instruction: See *differentiated instruction.*

Differentiated Instruction: A way of teaching that customizes the learning process to meet individual needs in whole-class and small-group instruction. In differentiated instruction, teachers have the option to make specific changes to content, teaching and learning processes, class materials, classroom management, and types of student assessment.

Division Facts: Division problems whose dividends are whole numbers between

Dividend
Divisor
Quotient

$16 \div 8 = 2$
$20 \div 4 = 5$

1 through 100 as well as extenders such as 1000, whose divisors are whole numbers between 0 and 10, and whose quotients are whole numbers without a remainder. Examples: $100 \div 4 = 25$, $1000 \div 10 = 100$, and $30 \div 5 = 6$.

Executive Function: Set of mental skills that help the brain organize and act on information; executive functioning skills are needed to make decisions, to solve problems, to manage emotions, to pay attention, to hold onto important information, to block out unnecessary information, as well as to prioritize and initiate tasks.

Experiential Learning: Learning through experience, or learning by reflecting on specific experiences. Developmental psychologist Jean Piaget theorized that children cannot learn that an oven is hot to the touch until they experience touching the hot oven themselves. The abstract concept of *hot* becomes concrete through experiential learning. See *kinesthetic learning.*

Expressive Language: Language that uses speech, writing, and nonverbal communication to convey thoughts and ideas. Nonverbal communication includes facial expressions and body language.

504 Plan: Once a learning disability has been identified that interferes with the student's ability to learn, a 504 Plan may be created in order to support the student's specific needs. A 504 Plan provides accommodations that help students succeed in the classroom without changing the curriculum. For example, if a student has a disability that affects his or her ability to focus, a 504 Plan accommodation could include preferential seating where the student sits close to the teacher. The 504 Plan is named for Section 504 of the Rehabilitation Act of 1973, which is a federal law that protects people with disabilities from discrimination.

Figure-Ground: The ability to distinguish an object from its background. This ability is important in recognizing surfaces, shapes, and objects.

Framework: An organized plan that determines the content students are expected to learn.

Franklin Spellers®: A particular brand of an electronic handheld tool that helps people correct their spelling errors. For example, a child may type *juraf,* and the speller will present phonetic alternatives (giraffe).

Higher-Order Reading Skills: Higher-order reading skills include higher-order thinking skills that allow for summarization, predictions, deductive reasoning, and inferences. These aptitudes assist readers to 'read between the lines' and glean important information.

IDEA: See *Individuals with Disabilities Education Act*

IEP: See *Individualized Education Program.*

Individualized Education Program (IEP): When a student is diagnosed with a learning disability, an IEP provides individualized education services to meet the student's unique needs. The federal special education law for children with disabilities, also known as the Individuals with Disabilities Education Act (IDEA), lists 13 specific disabilities that affect a person's ability to learn and perform.

Individuals with Disabilities Education Act (IDEA): A federal law that requires schools to serve the educational needs of eligible children with disabilities.

Inferential Analysis: Inferential analysis refers to the ability to use context clues to make an educated guess about a particular situation. This is an important skill for reading comprehension because it allows students to make predictions and draw conclusions.

Information Overload: People who experience information overload feel overwhelmed and struggle to learn and apply new concepts when they receive too much information in too little time.

Kinesthetic: Pertaining to movement.

Kinesthetic Learning: Hands-on learning style in which learning takes place by the students carrying out physical activities, rather than listening to a lecture or observing demonstrations. Kinesthetic learning can also be referred to as *experiential learning* because physical activity is an integral part of both experiences.

Linguistic Input: With regard to receptive language, linguistic input is the information a person receives from verbal, written, and nonverbal interactions.

Linguistic Output: With regard to expressive language, linguistic output is the information a person expresses in verbal, written, and nonverbal interactions.

Listening Comprehension: A process that occurs in the brain that allows people to understand spoken language and make meaning out of what they hear.

Long-term Memory: A vast store of knowledge and recall of information over a long period of time.

Lower-Order Reading Skills: Lower-order reading skills including basic skills such as recalling, memorizing, decoding, and repeating words, phrases, and passages.

Lunch Bunch Group: A group led by the school psychologist or social worker during the lunch period that includes children experiencing issues such as death, divorce, illness, bullying, and immature social judgment.

Main Idea and Supporting Details: The main idea is what the story is about. The supporting details add information to help the reader make sense or enhance the meaning of the main idea.

Manipulatives: Objects that students could touch and move around in order to learn new concepts. For example, match fact or color-coded cards to learn unit vocabulary terms and corresponding definitions.

Mathematical Conceptual Understanding: The profound understanding of mathematical ideas that allow students to build new knowledge from previously known information and experiences and be able to apply this knowledge to different situations and contexts.

Meaningful Learning: An approach to learning in which learned information is deeply understood, which allows the new material to be used to make connections with previously known knowledge.

Mental Flexibility: The ability to shift our attention fluidly in response to specific situations or demands as applied in different settings.

Mental Manipulation of Information: The ability to envision images from spoken or written language.

Modalities: Modalities refer to how students use their senses in the learning process. We commonly consider four modalities: visual (seeing), auditory (hearing), kinesthetic (moving), and tactile (touching).

Modifications: A term used in an Individualized Education Program (IEP) to indicate an element that changes what a student is taught or is expected to learn. For example, if a student has a reading issue, she might read a simplified version of the text. Students who receive modifications are not expected to learn the same material as their classmates due to their disability. See *accommodations.*

Motor Skills: The ability to move muscles precisely to perform a specific act. Motor skills are divided into two types: *fine motor skills* and *gross motor skills.* Fine motor skills control precision of small muscle movements while gross motor skills involve large muscle groups. Examples of fine motor skills are tying shoes and writing, while examples of gross motor skills are running and jumping.

Multiplication Facts: Multiplication problems whose factors are from 0 through 10 as well as extensions with multiples of 10 such as 100, 1000, etc. Examples:

$3 \times 9 = 27$, $40 \times 9 = 360$, and

$9 \times 2000 = 18,000$.

Factors	Product
$6 \times 6 = 36$	
$400 \times 9 = 3600$	

Multisensory Approach: Using two or more of the five traditional senses—vision, hearing, taste, smell, and touch—to enhance learning.

Para-professional: Members of the school staff who assist with teaching and monitoring for safety concerns. Para-professionals are commonly referred to as *paras*.

Parameters: In the case of behaviors and academic expectations, parameters refer to boundaries or limits.

Perceptual Development: An aspect of cognitive development that allows for interpretation and understanding of sensory information. The five senses allow for sensory input and our ability to increase perceptual development.

Phonemes: The basic sounds of a language that allow us to distinguish one word from another. Examples: the /k/, /s/, and /m/ as in the English language words *cat, sat,* and *mat.*

Process-Oriented Test: A test where students extrapolate information to answer a question. The SATs are process-oriented tests.

Product-Oriented Test: A test that focuses on specific content-based knowledge. The ACTs are product-oriented tests.

Pull-out: Students leave their classes to receive specific support by identified specialists who help them to develop skills in order to succeed within the general education curriculum.

Push-in: Specialists who come into classrooms to support students in core academic subjects. These specialists help students to succeed in the general education curriculum through small-group and one-on-one instruction.

Reading Comprehension: The process that students use to read, understand, and interpret information.

Reading with Expression: The ability to show feeling when reading. Reading with expression requires readers to read accurately, fluently, and with inflection and intonation as well as understanding text clues such as correct punctuation. For example, exclamation points indicate to readers that they should read with excitement, while question marks indicate that readers should use an inquisitive voice.

Receptive Language: Receptive language refers to people's ability to make interpretations based on verbal, nonverbal, and written information they receive from environmental interaction.

Restorative Justice: Making amends for inappropriate actions or behaviors. The goal of restorative justice is to repair students' standing in the community so they can move forward with their peers.

Retrieval: The process of recalling information when it is needed.

Right-Left Directionality Problems: Children are unable to discern their right from their left. This difficulty makes learning to read and write extremely difficult. Spatial relations, language, and quantity can cause reversals, memory problems, and confusion. (Source: Richard Cooper, learningdifferences.com)

Rote Learning: Learning information through the process of repetition and memorization. For example, for students who struggle with math, they may have to memorize basic math facts through rote learning.

Rote Memorization: Memorizing information through the process of repetition. See *rote learning.*

Scaffolding: Scaffolding refers to a variety of instructional techniques that add to the instruction. Scaffolding is used to move students progressively toward stronger understanding and, ultimately, greater independence in the learning process. An example of scaffolding includes building upon previously presented material in a concrete manner.

Scanning: Reading quickly over the whole page in search of a specific piece of information.

Self-control: The ability to self-regulate your own emotions, behavior, and actions and to control compulsive reactions.

Sentence: A thought that contains a subject and a verb.

Sentence Expanders: Modifiers added on to a basic sentence (called a *kernal sentence*) that increases the length and descriptions of sentences beyond a subject and a verb. For example, *The girls danced* is a basic or kernal sentence as it does not have modifiers. Adding modifiers such as *who, what, when, where, why,* and *how* expands the kernal sentence. The sentence *The girls danced at their recital yesterday* adds the modifiers where and when, allowing the reader to understand where and when the girls danced.

Short-term Memory: The mind's ability to recall information for a limited period of time.

Sight Read: Instant visual recognition of words.

Skill Base: Skill base refers to skills that are mastered and that demonstrate knowledge and competence in a specific area.

Skimming: Reading a text quickly to get the main idea of a story.

Smash the Task: A common expression used by teachers and tutors to break long-term assignments down into manageable components.

Social Cues: Signals people express and receive through verbal and nonverbal language; understanding social cues is necessary to understand people and navigate social situations. Social cues are culturally based. In Western cultures, for example, maintaining eye contact is socially appropriate and desirable, whereas in Asian cultures, it might be a sign of disrespect to maintain eye contact in conversation.

Social-Emotional Development: People's ability to understand their own feelings, manage their emotions, self-regulate their behavior, and form relationships.

Spatial Relationships: The ability to orient one's body in space and to perceive the positions of objects in relation to oneself and to other objects. In other words, it is the ability to understand the relationships of objects within the environment. Students with spatial relationship issues have difficulty with positions of multiple objects such as *next to, in front of, in back of, within, overlaps, crosses,* and *touches.*

Story Maps: A visual aid that allows students to visualize elements of a story, such as characters and plot.

Subtraction Facts: Subtraction problems whose minuends are whole numbers from 0 through 20 as well as their extenders (e.g., numbers such as 100 and 1000) and whose subtrahends are whole numbers from 0 through 10. Examples: $100 - 80 = 20$, $10 - 10 = 0$, and $9 - 3 = 6$.

Minuend —
Subtrahend —
Difference —

$4 - 3 = 1$
$15 - 8 = 7$

Syntax: The grammatical structure of sentences.

Tactile: Pertaining to the sense of touch.

Visual: Pertaining to the sense of sight.

Visual Aids: Objects, pictures, graphics, paintings, photographs, videos, and films that help increase a student's understanding of written or spoken information.

Visual Closure: The ability to identify incomplete figures when only fragments are presented. A person needs to see the parts of the whole as a complete unit.

Visual Discrimination: The ability to discriminate dominant features in different objects. Examples of dominant features include position, geometric-shaped forms, and letter-like forms. Students with visual discrimination issues may have difficulties seeing the subtle differences in objects of similar shapes or objects in unusual positions.

Visual Graphic Organizers: A tool used to visually structure and demonstrate relationships among facts, concepts, and ideas. (Source: LDAamerica.org)

Visual Memory: A form of memory and the ability to recall dominant features that are visually obtained and experienced.

Visual Perception: How visual information is processed and organized in the brain. Visual perception is different from visual acuity, which refers to how well a person sees.

Visual Problem Solving: The ability to identify and solve problems by creating visual images, using manipulatives, creating tables, organizing data, identifying and discerning differences in patterns, or by other concrete visible solutions.

Word Bank: Word banks are collections of terms and definitions displayed on a bulletin board in the classroom or students have their own collections written in their personal dictionaries on paper or electronically. Word banks are commonly used to assist with incorporating unit vocabulary in written responses and on exams. With English language learners and in heritage speaker language classrooms, word banks may also include audio recordings and visual images such as photographs or short videos.

Working Memory: Working memory is a type of short-term memory that allows us to retain and manipulate distinct pieces of information for a matter of seconds.

Organizations and Community Resources

Anxiety and Depression Association of America (ADAA)

 adaa.org

f @AnxietyAndDepressionAssociationOfAmerica

t @Got_Anxiety

📞 (240) 485-1001

✉ 8701 Georgia Avenue, Suite 412, Silver Springs, MD 20910

"ADAA is an international nonprofit organization dedicated to the prevention, treatment, and cure of anxiety, depressive, obsessive-compulsive, and trauma-related disorders through education, practice, and research."

Attention Deficit Disorder Association (ADDA)

 add.org

f @ADHDAdult

t @adultadhd

"The ADDA is the world's leading adult ADHD program. Since its inception, ADDA has become the source for information and resources exclusively for and about adult ADHD. The transition from high school to post-secondary education is traditionally a difficult step, fraught with challenges and roadblocks for adults with ADHD. Students with ADHD are more likely to struggle with academic under-achievement. That is why ADDA has endeavored to ease this transition by developing programming exclusively for post-secondary students. ADDA's dedicated professionals routinely provide information and strategies so that adults with ADHD don't just survive in school, but thrive there."

The Association of Boarding Schools (TABS)

 TABS.org

@boardingschool

 @TABSorg

(828) 258-5354

One North Pack Square, Suite 301, Ashville, NC 28801

"The Association of Boarding Schools serves college-preparatory boarding schools in the United States, Canada, and around the globe. The Association leads a domestic and international effort to promote awareness and understanding of boarding schools and to expand the applicant pool for member institutions."

California Association for Bilingual Education (CABE)

 gocabe.org

f @cabeorg

t @CABEBEBILINGUAL

📞 (626) 814-4441

✉ 16033 East San Bernardino Road, Covina, CA 91722-3900

"CABE is a non-profit organization incorporated in 1976 to promote bilingual education and quality educational experiences for all students in California. CABE has 5,000 members and a total of over 30 chapters, affiliates, and partnerships with other state and national advocacy organizations, all working to promote equity and student achievement for students with diverse cultural, racial, and linguistic backgrounds. CABE recognizes and honors the fact that we live in a rich multicultural, global society and that respect for diversity makes us a stronger state and nation."

Child Mind Institute

 childmind.org

f @ChildMindInstitute

t @ChildMindDotOrg

📞 (212) 308-3118

✉ 445 Park Avenue, New York, NY 10022

"We are an independent nonprofit dedicated to transforming the lives of children struggling with mental health and learning disorders."

College Success Plan

 collegesuccessplan.com

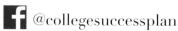 @collegesuccessplan

@EmpowerCSP

℡ 630-481-6153

"College Success Plan mentors help students apply appropriate and efficient learning strategies that keep them on track through what is today a rigorous and demanding college life."

College Supports for Learning Differences (CSLD)

collegesupports.com

℡(847) 940-8090

"College Supports for Learning Differences' mission is to provide detailed descriptions of services available, personnel providing the service, contact persons at each institution, and costs to the students as reported directly from service providers."

Common Sense Media

🌐 commonsensemedia.org

f @commonsensemedia

t @commonsense

📞 (415) 863-0600

✉ 650 Townsend, Suite 435, San Francisco, CA 94103

"Common Sense Media is a San Francisco based non-profit organization that provides education and advocacy to families to promote safe technology and media for children."

Council for Exceptional Children (CEC)

🌐 cec.sped.org

f @cechq

t @CECMembership

📞 (888) 232-7733

✉ 2900 Crystal Drive, Arlington, VA 22202

"The Council for Exceptional Children is the largest international professional organization dedicated to improving the educational success of individuals with disabilities and/or gifts and talents."

Council for Learning Disabilities

🌐 Council-for-learning-disabilities.org

ⓔ @CLDIntl

📞 (913) 491-1011

✉️ 11184 Antioch Road, Box 405, Overland Park, KS 66210

The Council for Learning Disabilities is an international organization composed of professionals from multiple disciplines. It promotes evidence-based research and practices related to the education of individuals with learning disabilities. "We foster collaboration among professionals, developmental leaders in the field, and advocacy for policies that support individuals with learning disabilities at local, state, and national levels."

Eye to Eye

🌐 eyetoeyenational.org

📘 @eyetoeyenational

ⓔ @E2ENational

📞 (212) 537-4429

✉️ 50 Broad Street, Suite 1702, New York, NY 10004

Eye to Eye's mission is to improve the life of every person with a learning disability. "We fulfill our mission by supporting and growing a network of youth mentoring programs run by and for those with learning differences, and by organizing advocates to support the full inclusion of people with learning disabilities and ADHD in all aspects of society."

Greenwood Associates, Inc.

(An international Career and Educational Counseling Group)

 greenwdassoc.com

@greenwdassoc

(213) 261-6418

288 Beach Drive NE #7A, St. Petersburg, FL 33701

By taking The GS-120 or GS 45, an individual's natural abilities, interests, personalities and values/lifestyles can be identified with this online tool and will make appropriate career choices apparent. A career guidance tool can help to foster smart education decisions, identify the right internships, build a resume of relevant accomplishments, and find a job right out of high school or college. Crossroads are always challenging, and transitioning from one phase to another poses a certain level of uncertainty. Being able to identify college and career paths greatly reduces the level of uncertainty and helps to define how best to obtain the education or specific skill set needed to secure future employment.

Independent Educational Consultants Association (IECA)

🌐 iecaonline.com

f @IECA.IndependentEducationalConsultantsAssn

t @ieca

📞 (703) 591-4850

✉ 3251 Old Lee Highway, Suite 510, Fairfax, VA 22030

"IECA promotes the highest quality independent educational consulting to students and families seeking skilled, ethical, academic, or therapeutic guidance; to enhance professional development; and to foster career satisfaction among members."

Learning Disabilities Association of America

🌐 ldaamerica.org

f @LDAAmerica

t @LDAofAmerica

📞 (212) 924-8896

✉ 237 W 35th Street, New York, NY 10001

"LDA provides support to people with learning disabilities, their parents, teachers, and other professionals with cutting edge information on learning disabilities."

National Association for Bilingual Education (NABE)

🌐 nabe.org

f @nabeorg

t @NABEorg

📞 (240) 450-3700

✉ 11006 Veirs Mills Road, L-1 Wheaton, MD 20902

"The National Association for Bilingual Education (NABE) is a non-profit membership organization that works to advocate for educational equity and excellence for bilingual/multilingual students in a global society. NABE supports the education of English Language learners. By using native and second languages in everyday life, we not only develop intercultural understanding, but we also show by example that we respect and can effectively cross cultural and linguistic borders."

National Association for the Education of Young Children

🌐 naeyc.org

f @NAEYC

t @NAEYC

📞 (202) 232-8777, (800) 424-2460

✉ 1313 L St NW, Suite 500, Washington, DC 20005

For updated online publications concerning questions and concerns about policies, development for professionals and parents interested in helping dual language learners succeed in academic settings.

National Association of Therapeutic Schools and Programs (NATSAP)

 natsap.org

 @NATSAPDC

@NATSAPDC

📞 (301) 986-8770

✉ 5272 River Road, Suite 600, Bethesda, MD 20816

"NATSAP serves as an advocate and resource for innovative organizations which devote themselves to society's need for the education of struggling young people and their families."

National Center for Learning Disabilities (NCLD)

 ncld.org

@ncldorg

@ncldorg

✉ 32 Laight Street, Second Floor, New York, NY 10013

"Our mission is to improve the lives of the 1 in 5 children and adults nationwide with learning and attention issues—by empowering parents and young adults."

Reading Rockets

- readingrockets.org
- @ReadingRockets.org
- @ReadingRockets
- 2775 S. Quincy St., Arlington, VA 22206

"Reading Rockets is a national multimedia project that offers a wealth of research-based reading strategies, lessons, and activities designed to help young children learn how to read and read better. Our reading resources assist parents, teachers, and other educators in helping struggling readers build fluency, vocabulary, and comprehension skills."

Understood (Learning and Attention Issues)

- understood.org
- @Understood
- @UnderstoodOrg

"15 nonprofit organizations have joined forces to support parents of the one and five children with learning and attention issues throughout their journey. With the right support, parents can help children unlock their strengths and reach their full potential. With state-of-the-art technology, personalized resources, free daily access to experts, a secure online community, practical tips and more, Understood aims to be that support."

U.S. Department of Education

 ed.gov

 @ED.gov

 @usedgov

Contact education agencies in your state including your state's Department of Education as well as their different departments. According to the U.S. Department of Education, "Our mission is to promote student achievement and preparation for global competitiveness by fostering educational excellence and ensuring equal access."

Index

About the Author

Dana Stahl is a learning specialist, educational consultant, and advocate for children and their parents. She earned a Bachelor of Science degree from Boston University in Special Education and a Master of Education degree in Diagnostic/Prescriptive Teaching from the College of William and Mary.

In 2005, Dana developed a private practice in Katonah, New York, working directly with children ages four to 18 on developing their academic skill set and preparing them for their next educational crossroad. Dana's in-depth background in the field of learning disabilities affords her the opportunity to provide a wide array of academic interventions.

As a child, Dana experienced learning issues firsthand. Before she was diagnosed, she struggled to convey her challenges with her teachers and family. In first grade in 1966, three years after dyslexia was an officially recognized diagnosis, Dana was placed in the untenable position of having to demonstrate that she was bright, competent, and capable even though reading was nearly impossible.

As an educator and advocate, she understands the concerns parents have with their children's academic performance. She knows what they are going through and the frustration and anxiety that parents and their children are experiencing because she had to deal with her own profound learning disabilities.

As a learning specialist, Dana regularly reads psychoeducational and neuropsychoeducational evaluations of students and then writes a summary of the students' strengths and vulnerabilities, assessing whether their educational profiles are an appropriate match to the curricular demands of the schools to which they are applying.

Dana accompanies parents to CSE meetings and fights for the rights of children to receive appropriate classifications and accommodations. On behalf of her clients, she also petitions the College Board and ACT for specific accommodations on PSATs, SATs, and ACTs.

Dana is a member of the Independent Education Consultant Association (IECA), the National Association of Therapeutic Schools and Programs (NATSAP), and the Council for Exceptional Children (CEC). Dana is on the Board of Directors of Thistlewaithe Learning Center, a Montessori school for children ages three to six in Westchester County, New York. Since 2014, Dana has visited over 100 schools that offer special learning environments. She can help parents find appropriate programs and placements for their child, adolescent or young adult, identifying placements in LD day schools, boarding schools, postgraduate, and gap year programs as well as colleges with LD support. She can then secure the placement by working closely with families, counselors and learning specialists to assure a successful admission to a supportive social-emotional and educational environment.

Dana's observations in visiting these schools enables her to ascertain the gap between home and school communication due largely to the schools' inability to adequately describe students' learning issues in a clear and concise manner. Dana also realizes that oftentimes parents are challenged by their inability to articulate their children's academic, behavioral, and social-emotional observations. To address these needs, Dana created *The ABCs of Learning Issues* for parents and *BOXES* for educators.

With Dana's vast personal and professional experiences, she can assure that her clients receive sound educational advice, advocacy, and placement. Dana's commitment to helping children at various stages of their lives allows her to guide parents in assisting their children through their educational journey.

The ABCs of Learning Issues along with its companion guide BOXES bridges the gap between the school and the home by demystifying the areas of concerns educators observe in school and parents witness at home.

BOXES stands for **Better Organization and Xplanations of Exceptional Students.** It is designed for educators and paraprofessionals who will benefit from an in-depth understanding of issues and behaviors described in psychoeducational and neuropsychological evaluations. It also addresses differential instruction for educators creating the opportunity for all students to reach their academic potential. BOXES includes:

- An explanation of commonly identified learning issues that are often observed but are regularly untreated in school settings
- Behaviors that educators observe in their students
- Effective teaching strategies including differential instruction for their students
- Blackline Masters with templates that facilitate home-school and intra-school communication

For more information on differentiated instruction for children with learning issues, go to EducationalAlternativesLLC.com.

For multilingual support, please visit PalmichePress.com.